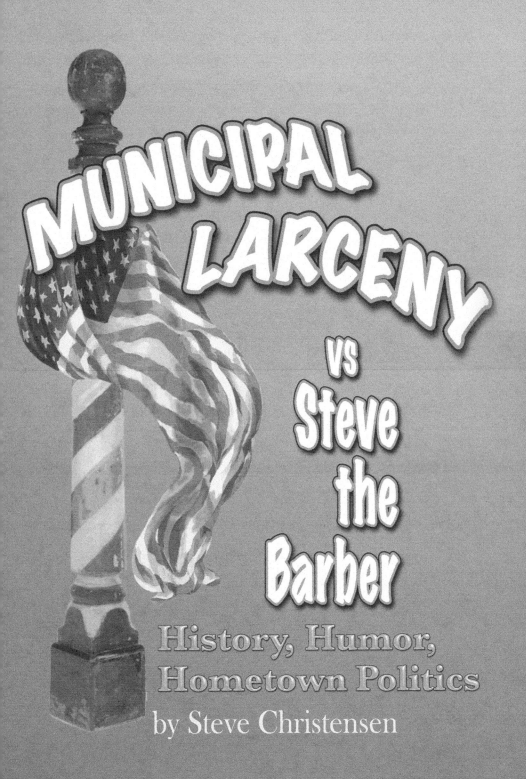

MUNICIPAL LARCENY

vs Steve the Barber

History, Humor, Hometown Politics

by Steve Christensen

Municipal Larceny vs Steve the Barber
©2021, Steve Christensen

ISBN: 978-1-09836-6-612
ISBN eBook: 978-1-09836-6-629

ACKNOWLEDGEMENTS

Family First:

Lorraine, *my best friend, my wife, recognizes both my strengths and weaknesses better than anyone. I rate my overblown sense of humor as a strength. Lorraine, who is much more sensitive to decorum and political correctness, than I, has had to step in and tone me down from time to time. She knows I find way too many things to be hilarious, which normal people label as crude, rude, obnoxious, or downright disgusting. I admit I've gotten myself in trouble because of it;*

Her sister, **Linda**, *and hubby,* **Robert Swanson**, *helped out with proof reading, provided the sketches, and helpful suggestions so even non-local readers could have a better understanding;*

Her brother **Tony French** *and his wife* **Michelle** *for being so very encouraging after reading a very rough first draft;*

Our daughter, **Connie Mancasola**, *hubby* **Matt**, *and grandson* **Mason**, *along with our son* **Joe** *and grandsons,* **Joey** *and* **Cole**, *all shared some valuable suggestions with us;*

Cousin **Dave Christensen**, *photography;*

* * * * * * * * * * * *

My good friend, **Mike Gilchrist**, *the workhorse, whose pleasure in life is helping out his friends. He created some covers, arranged the formatting and along with his wife,* **LeAnn**, *is responsible for a lot of the correct grammar. His career choice required top level computer expertise. I desperately needed help in that area. His efforts certainly saved me countless hours of frustration. I could not have gotten here without him;*

Another good friend, for over seventy years, for sharing and verifying some of the history ... **Dr. John Rivers**

THANKS TO ALL

TABLE OF CONTENTS

CHAPTER ONE

A Little History

It's been over thirty years since my very first visit to City Hall to speak at a City Council meeting. I had a complaint against one of our city's policies.

Before we get to the battles with City Hall, I want to give some history about myself and my town. Prior to that first trip to City Hall, I had already worked as a barber in our town for 28 years. When I got back home with my Barber License at the age of 18, I had no idea of the wonderful education in human nature which would be coming my way. In fifty-nine years, I went from being the youngest barber in town to the oldest.

As a barber, you get to hear it all. It's better than being a bartender. Sometimes a barber can go a week or two without having to suffer through any alcohol induced blathering. Don't get me wrong. I'm not saying that sober blathering is any more palatable.

One on one, private conversations with people from all segments of society truly gives one a great understanding of human nature.

Back to my early years. I landed a job in the biggest and busiest shop in town, Fischer's Barber Shop. Like a typical teenager, I had no interest whatsoever in politics. When either the City Mayor, or County Supervisor, or State Assemblyman, or Police Chief, or Sheriff, or District Attorney was in the shop, politics and newsworthy topics dominated the conversation. I would eavesdrop and sometimes try to pretend like I knew what they were talking about. Every once in a while when one of them was asked what the real story was, they'd say *You didn't hear this from me* and then go on to share a few tidbits, swearing us to secrecy. Sometimes the guy's picture was in the newspaper laying on the counter. So, I'd read the paper after he left. I didn't know if the newspaper left out the best part, or he just didn't tell them the same story he told us. My education was beginning.

I was only four years old when my folks moved us from the Los Angeles area to the small town of Oroville, in Northern California. Oroville sits where the Feather River flows from the hills into the valley. Several years of my childhood had passed before Oroville installed its first traffic signal.

I got my first and only bicycle at age seven. By the time I was twelve, that bike had seen every road within five miles of Oroville in all directions. Back in the fifties, kids on bikes were all over the place. After school let out, some boys had jobs peddling the local newspaper. They'd pick up their load of papers, put them in a canvas bag and race to the bars. Guys on barstools were big tippers. Sometimes they'd buy more than one paper.

Besides selling or delivering newspapers, there were many other jobs available for school kids. Every gas station hired youngsters. There were no self service gas stations back then. Customers were treated to windshield washing, tire pressure and oil level checks while the tank was filling. Many restaurants, grocery stores and timber fallers also hired young people.

I worked in agriculture, including harvesting of citrus, nuts, row crops and rice. My last two years of high school I had steady employment, real jobs with tax withheld from paychecks. A real boring job was flagging crop dusters. Before GPS guided the crop duster pilots, they had to depend on a flagman to move over 30 feet to get them on line for every pass.

A couple miles north of Oroville lies a flat top mountain appropriately named Table Mountain. It dominates the horizon. In 1929 some Oroville High School students hauled concrete and water up the slope and formed a giant O overlooking our town. In the fifties, my bike would get hidden in the brush at the base of the mountain. The hike up to the O was pretty easy for kids. Once you got past the O, and up to the flat top, there were miles and miles available for hiking. There are some canyons and creeks cutting through the flat mountain top. Swimming and drinking the creek water were part of every hike.

Table Mountain

The biggest high school sports rival of the day was Chico High School from our neighboring town to the Northwest. Before a football game between the two schools, some Chico kids went up Table Mountain, under the cover of darkness, and blacked out enough of the O to turn it into a C. Oroville kids didn't like it. The event sparked an annual tradition which lasted for many years. Sentries from Oroville High School would be assigned to camp all night to protect the O. Every year, the day after the battle for the O was over, it was the big story around the schoolyard. Even some of the teachers chimed in.

The Feather River separates the City of Oroville from the area across the river known as Thermalito. Bedrock Park, right on the river, was the best place to be all summer long for vacationing school-kids. Hundreds of us showed up daily. It was only a two mile bike ride from the house. Because there were no traffic signals and not much traffic, it was always a fast trip. Better yet, Grandma's house was only four blocks away from the swimming hole. She always had snacks. Some of the Thermalito kids showed up on the other side of the river. They would leave their bikes and swim over.

The other popular river swimming hole, Bidwell Bar, was a nine mile road trip up stream. That was a tough bike ride. My bike had no gears. Steep hills required walking the bike instead of riding it. I was glad when some of my older friends got cars.

In the fifties, cruising was the most popular thing high-schoolers did. You'd ride around in cars and wave at each other. You would park in Drive-ins, visit each other, set up drag races and hide the beer when the cops rolled in. There was a movie called **American Graffiti**. That movie really nailed it.

The fifties were the Golden Age of Automobiles. Every year all models of all makes of cars were not seen by the public until a scheduled day for the whole country. Trucks and trains which transported the new models had to keep them covered. Unlike today, you didn't have to look at the logo to tell what kind of car it was. Every year, every car had a new look. Downtown Oroville had several new car showrooms. Their windows would be papered and no one would be allowed in until the big day arrived. When the last bell rang at Oroville High School on *new car day* some of us ran to all the showrooms in town to see next year's models.

There was a Black neighborhood in Oroville. Before the term *African American* was thought up, people of African descent were called Negroes or Colored Folks. There was about a 30 block area, in *Southside* where they lived as neighbors. The first house my parents bought was on the borderline block. As a little kid I had no reason to know there was such a thing as racial prejudice. The *N word* never was dropped by my folks.

Most had migrated here from the southern states. With them came their southern lifestyles. Segregation had been the normal way of life in the South. Attending school was the first social-izing between the different races for most of us. The attraction which brought them here was the need for workers in agriculture and timber.

Oroville must have been a great environment for many of the people who grew up in those thirty blocks. One of my friends and classmates, Dr. John Rivers, chose to move home to Oroville after retiring from a career in education. He had been the Vice President of Hayward State University. After retirement, he formed the South Oroville African American Historical Society (SOAHHS). Since I went through grammar school as a Southside boy, he invited me to serve on the board. I was highly honored.

Dr. Rivers took boxing lessons as a young boy. He went on to win the NCAA boxing championship two years in a row as a Chico State College student. He also served as Vice President of Student Affairs. While in the US Army he won the all-services boxing championship.

Oroville High School had a boxing tournament in the fifties. I was a pretty good boxer in the PE class, so the coach encouraged me to sign up for the tournament. I asked him how much John Rivers weighed. He said 125. Since I weighed the same amount, I declined.

Many of the fine people who grew up in the thirty blocks went on to great things. Besides Dr. Rivers, I think Rear Admiral Robert Toney deserves marquee billing. As one of the first three black men to rise to the rank of Admiral in the history of the US Navy, his great-est responsibility was to oversee all US military facilities resources in the 100 million square mile Pacific Area from our West Coast all the way to the East Coast of Africa.

Other outstanding military accolades go to Colonel Fred Jones, the 43rd black officer in the history of the US Marine Corps who went on to mentor four future Marine Corps Generals. Captain Leroy Gill quit school to join the Navy and became the second black Captain in the history of the US Merchant Marines.

A couple of others from the Southside 30 square blocks made their marks in politics. Warren Widener served as a Captain in the US Air Force and after his military service ended, he settled in the San Francisco Bay Area and was the third black man to be elected to the Berkeley City Council. He later became the first black Mayor elected in Berkeley. He finished his political career as an Alameda County Supervisor. His wife, Mary Lee Widener, had a successful career in addressing housing needs for racial minorities and people of low income. Her efforts led to the National Conference 2000 Housing Person of the year Award. Coincidentally, Mary's brother, the late Mert Thomas, was the first black to be elected to Oroville City council and went on to serve as Vice-Mayor.

There were several Southside kids who grew up to receive paychecks from professional sports franchises. Football, basketball, and baseball all had players who had grown up within the thirty blocks. The only other athlete I'm going to mention by name, like John Rivers, was an amateur. Tennis was her game, Roz Bell was her name. She was World Champion in both singles and doubles for women over 75 in 2013 which helped her to reach number one world ranking in both categories.

Besides people of such lofty accomplishments, SOAAHS also include average folks in its quarterly *Southside Chronicle*. Dr. Rivers recruited me to write a story about Willie "Shorty" Hogan, a shoe shiner who worked at Fischer's Barber Shop much longer than I did. I'll recreate my story.

Willie "Shorty" Hogan Barbershop Stories

by Steve Christensen

I first saw Shorty back in '47 when I was a little kid and my Dad was a barber at Fischer's on Myers Street. I couldn't figure out why they called him Shorty, everyone looked big to me. Shorty had the shoe shine stand outside in front of the barber shop. His rent was paid by sweeping the floor and cleaning the ashtrays. Shoe shining was a step down from his previous occupation. Before the Great Depression he'd been a chef on a passenger train.

My favorite story of Shorty was told to me by my Dad in my first year of high school, 1956. The upcoming World Series featured a rematch between the champion Brooklyn Dodgers and the New York Yankees.

My Dad's customer said he would bet $500 the Dodgers would win again. Back in '56, $500 had the same buying power as $5000 today.

For a single dollar, one could buy a pack of smokes, a gallon of gas, a hamburger and a cup of coffee and still have some coins left over for his pocket. So $500 was big. Shorty whispered to my Dad, "Take the bet" and laid five $100 bills in his hand. My Dad threw the five bills in his customer's lap and said, "You got a bet, put up your money." The customer was bluffing and got called. My Dad said the guy's jaw dropped, he shook his head and never said another word for the duration of his haircut. Shorty would have won the bet.

In '62 I worked at Fischer's Barber Shop. Shorty was still there. Every day he would buy a pint of Walker's DeLuxe whiskey. Downtown Oroville had a couple of liquor stores then. If Shorty was gone a few minutes, he always had a brown paper sack when he returned. The sack would go in the drawer below the foot racks of the shoe shine stand. He never left the sack in the stand if he had to leave again. He would hide the sack in the barber shop back closet.

Some days he would ask for a ride home. If he hadn't got the sack in town he'd ask me if we could stop at Pigg's Liquor Store before I dropped him off at his home on Florence Ave.

One day he'd bought his jug in town and hid it in the closet. He used a new hiding place. At closing time he went to the closet to retrieve the jug, he looked in his usual hiding place and it was not there. He accused Otis, the barber, of stealing his whiskey. Otis was a World War 2 vet who had endured 11 days without sleep due to constant artillery explosions. Otis got drunk twice a day. So Shorty figured he was the most likely suspect. Shorty asked Otis if he'd taken his whiskey. Otis was outraged and said, "If I took your whiskey I'll kiss your black *'backside' and I can assure you it is black." Back then, I was a bit of an agitator and asked Otis, "How do you know what color his 'backside' is?" Otis said, "You skinny punk, I'll KICK your white 'backside."' Even though Otis had a big beer gut and weighed close to 300, I'd seen him win many one dollar bets by kicking the door header which was over six feet above the floor. He could have kicked me through the roof. I decided to refrain from any further agitating. On the way home, Shorty asked me, "How does he know what color your 'backside' is?" We both laughed all the way to Florence Ave.*

Back in the middle or late sixties, Marcellus Smith told me Shorty moved to Texas to live with a niece for the rest of his days.

Prior to American black folks finding their way to Oroville, there also had been a significant number of immigrants from China. It has been estimated there were up to 10,000 Chinese here at one time. One of Oroville's museums is a Chinese Temple which is listed on the National Registry of Historical Places. The city took it over in the 1930s. It's both a museum and an active temple, occasionally used for worship.

The first attraction for the Chinese to come here was the California Gold Rush, and later came a need for railroad construction workers. There are still some residents here who are descendants of the earliest immigrants.

Oroville's history, from its beginning, is of short booms, followed by long busts.

The first, most explosive boom began in the fall of 1849 when pick and shovel gold miners flocked here for the easy pickin's. Gold was plentiful, but food and supplies were not. When the mud which came with winter rains made wagon travel impossible, men could profit by backpacking supplies in on foot. Everything sold for $1.25 a pound, except for whiskey which garnered a much higher price.

By 1856 Oroville boasted the fifth largest population in California of over 4,000 people. The same year Oroville applied to be incorporated as a city.

After a few short years the first boom was ending. The days of the individual miners washing one pan at a time were coming to an end. Because of high demand, some individual claims were as small as 100 square feet. Miners formed friendships and teamed up. Mining had evolved into partnerships. The partners could work multiple claims. The use of rockers, long toms and sluice boxes replaced the gold pan. The easy gold had already been harvested. The pick and shovel miners moved on when rumors of gold in other states reached town. In 1859 Oroville disincorporated as a city because of the shrinking population. In a one year span half the population had left. Corporations were taking over the gold recovery business. They hired employees and the Wall Street type investors raked in the profits. One investor was Herbert Hoover who later became President of the United States. Inventor Thomas Edison also invested.

Hydraulic mining techniques were developed. Diversion dams, flumes, ditches and pipes had to be constructed to deliver the water to rich mining sites. The town of Cherokee, north of Oroville, had the biggest hydraulic mine in operation. A hundred miles of flumes, ditches, and thirty inch pipes were built for the Cherokee mine. When the water reached the mine, hoses with nozzles called monitors directed nine inch streams of water toward the earth from as far as 400 feet away and ate it away. The Cherokee mine had eighteen of these working. The earth, rocks and water would be delivered to sluice boxes to recover the gold. Nine miles of sluice boxes were used to catch gold. They also mined diamonds. United States President Rutherford Hayes visited the mine. This mine used three times as much water as the entire city of San Francisco. After several years, California outlawed hydraulic mining because of the ugly scarring of the earth.

The first ever gold dredge in the world was built in Oroville in 1877. It took some trial and error to make dredging profitable. Successful dredges were large machines which floated on pontoons. As they improved they were outfitted with bucket ladders which brought the earth up to be dumped on a wash line and forced the heavier gold to sink to the bottom. The lighter dirt and rocks went off the other end on a rotating belt and were known as tailings.

Besides dredges being placed in rivers, they could also operate in moving ponds by excavating all the ground which was reachable and then move forward. The tailings belt would backfill the gap they had just dug. The pond moved with them. Six thousand acres of dredger tailings and ugly rows of river rock lied on the outskirts of Oroville for over fifty years.

Agriculture and logging were waiting in line to remove mining from the list of the top industry in the area. It would take until the 1900s before Oroville's population steadied and then began to increase again. Busts last about ten times as long as booms.

Every 50 to 60 years Oroville has another boom. The Feather River was also the reason there was a second boom. The price gouging which Central Pacific Railroad enjoyed because of its monopoly on rail travel justified the creation of a competitive train route. For over thirty years the owners of the Central Pacific succeeded in delaying the project. They didn't want the competition. An ideal one percent grade could be maintained for a railroad constructed through the Feather River canyon. The highest elevation the new railroad would have to deal with was more than two thousand feet lower than the existing route over Donner Pass.

In 1903 the Western Pacific Railroad was incorporated. The boom began slowly. The first couple of years there was no tsunami of men eager to build a railroad as there was who showed up for the gold rush. Laborers were hard to come by. The solution was to offer high wages which attracted workers from around the globe. Also, some nefarious types who were fugitives from the law and couldn't hang around the towns which were looking for them, showed up. Crime in Oroville increased. Western Pacific caught a break in 1907 when a national business downturn occurred.

The tsunami started when men needed work. Wages dropped. The old abandoned mining camps in the Feather River canyon, from the gold rush days were revived. Oroville became an incorporated city again. Whiskey merchants thrived again. In 1910 the first passenger train used the new route, welcomed by celebrations all along the way.

The third boom, right on schedule, lasted from 1962 until 1968. The Feather River gets the credit again. Oroville Dam was constructed during this time. The plan was for the nation's highest dam to be built to capture the 3,600 square miles of watershed. The six thousand acres of dredger tailings were finally put to good use. They were used to build the dam. Trains were used to haul the material to the dam site which was a few miles upstream from the town of Oroville. The water was to be sent to thirsty Southern California while simultaneously turning turbines to produce electrical power. The first year of the boom, I hadn't quite reached the age to legally drink, gamble, or vote. Back then, I was really only interested in doing the first two. In twelve square blocks of downtown Oroville there were eighteen bars. Outside of the downtown area there were probably more than eighteen others.

I've always been a bit of a history buff. Around twelve years ago, through the barbershop window, I saw a well dressed couple park a luxury vehicle sporting out of state plates in my parking lot. They both came in to ask me some questions. He said he lived here as a school kid when the family moved to Oroville because construction workers were needed for the Oroville Dam. Forty years after leaving, he was back.

After a successful career, he wanted to start off retirement by writing a book about his life. He had finished his first year of high school here when the dam was completed back in 1968. The family then had to move on to the next job. He wanted to include a chapter or two in his book about his school days in Oroville. He said my name came up when he asked several people around town if they knew anybody who had lived here a long time and knew a lot of the local history.

When he asked if I knew a lot of the history, I answered, "- Know it? I invented about half of it." His wife cracked up. We hit it off really well. We had a couple of long visits, lunched together, and I gave them a tour. I told him I would be interested in reading his book. When he left town, he had my phone number and address.

We exchanged a few letters. He admitted to being stuck in the mud with some *writers cramp* and his book was not moving forward at all because of his travels abroad. I e-mailed him recently and asked about his book. If he followed through and finished it, I was hoping to get a few pointers. I haven't heard back yet.

Oroville was chosen by some Hollywood film companies for movie productions a few times. It seems it was 1973, maybe '74, production crew and cast members came to town to do a movie titled *The Klansman*. There were high hopes of a future blockbuster, as the cast consisted of some of the top stars of the day. Richard Burton, accompanied by Elizabeth Taylor, along with Lee Marvin, and rookie actor, O. J. Simpson were the marquee names.

The casting director recruited me and another local barber, as extras, to be in the barber shop scene. I learned film making can be very boring. There is a lot of down time between takes which allows idle conversation to consume much more time than actual filming. Richard Burton loved chatting with the extras. Rumor has it he could swig down a couple quarts of hard liquor every day. Lee Marvin could match him drink for drink.

The booze didn't seem to affect Burton much. He told us he once won a $25,000 bet by reciting every single word of every single part of the play **Hamlet**, BACKWARDS.

The director, Terrence Young, like Burton, also was British. His claim to fame came from his efforts in directing some early *James Bond* movies. He instructed me to say a single line, *Thank you Mr. Taggert.* I didn't know at the time, if extras spoke a single word they would qualify as an actor and receive much higher pay. There are also lifetime royalties triggered by every viewing of the movie.

Young told me, "Get more snappy when removing the hair cloth, over on the Continent barbers do it like this." He grabbed the hair cloth out of my hand, gave it a few whip snaps while jumping up and down. I'd never seen anything like it. I thought if I did that at my shop, all the waiting customers would flee.

Having spent some time in the South in military uniform, prior to integration kicking in, I thought Young might appreciate some insight about the southern lifestyle.

I told him I thought we were supposed to portray the good old boys from the South, they have a slow drawl, tobacco juice running down the chin, and everywhere they go it's in slow motion. He didn't bother to thank me, but he left me alone from then on. I later wished I had just followed the director's wishes. Maybe he would have notified the paymaster he had promoted me to a speaking part. I could have smart-mouthed myself out of a bigger payday.

The financiers of the production were not experienced in film making. It appeared to me, the Hollywood people all knew it, and seized the opportunity have a fun time and get paid for partying.

The movie turned out to be a bust. If you watch the whole thing, you will very likely say it is the worse movie you ever saw.

CHAPTER TWO

Barbershop Americana

In 1963 I had become of age. I got hired by my Dad to run his small one man Barber Shop. One could exit through the back of the shop and pass through one of Oroville's eighteen bars. Lots of my customers liked waiting for their turn while sitting at the bar. Some, who weren't even my customers, used the Barber Shop front door just to access the bar. Maybe they didn't want people to know their real destination. Every eight hours, hundreds of men got off work and most of them went to a watering hole or two. The graveyard shift would get to town a little after eight in the morning. When I opened at 9:00 AM the party was well under way. Wives and girlfriends would already be feeling the effects and singing and dancing.

The funniest thing I remember happening at the shop was when a daily bar customer came in after over indulging. He pointed at his hair and asked me to shave it all off and put it in a paper bag. I was a little curious but did not ask why. He volunteered anyway, telling me he needed to teach that *B-word* a lesson. She was in the same condition as he was and had told him the only thing she liked about him was his curly hair. I followed him and his bag back to the bar and watched him throw his hair all over the girlfriend yelling, "Here you go *B-word*, if that's what you like you got it!" The next morning when they came in he was wearing a new hat, and they were happily back to partying as usual.

Six of the downtown bars had poker tables. There were times every seat at every poker table was filled and every bar stool had a set of cheeks on it. Bartenders all had new cars. Drunk driving tickets were rarely given. Only drunks who became defiant when pulled over put themselves at risk of arrest. Guys would stop in the Barber Shop and ask if I knew where they'd parked their car.

Most transient construction workers were forced to buy homes because of the lower cost of making payments versus paying rent. When the job ended the workers left town and mortgage lenders ended up with a very large inventory of foreclosures. Oroville returned to normal, higher than average unemployment, and lower than average household income. It lasted for almost fifty years until the next boom hit.

2017, right on schedule, the mighty Feather River seemed to make up for five years of drought in several weeks. The lake level set a new record. It exceeded capacity. The spillway of Oroville Dam failed. More than 180,000 downstream residents were ordered to evacuate for fear the dam itself could fail. The boom immediately followed. Many out of town construction workers found their way to Oroville once more. Many local people got high paying jobs. Restaurants and casinos prospered. The City of Oroville vastly exceeded revenue projections because of the business spike. As the spillway repair wound down a year and a half later, the Camp Fire consumed the neighboring town of Paradise. Oroville's population grew by four thousand. The continuing business spike was even more beneficial to the city coffers.

The 1% sales tax increase the voters blessed the city with, had already kicked in. If things stay true to form the next boom should be due around 2070.

I am now in my sixtieth year of standing behind the iron chair. After eight weeks of social distancing because of Covid 19, I decided to try my hand at writing a book.

My all-time single favorite barbershop story is about a local character we called Big D. Big D passed away at age 63 early in 2020. I had been his off and on barber since he was a school kid. His young life was very checkered. His Dad was always drunk when he wasn't at work. I didn't remember ever knowing his Dad. Big D had a younger brother and sister. Their Mom was a shoplifter. She would create a ruckus with the smaller kids in the stroller to distract the store employees. When Big D was still a Little D, his job was to snatch and hide the items she wanted and head out the door. He was still a Little D when she and the younger kids disappeared. He was uncontrolled, almost on his own, at a very young age. He developed a weakness for controlled substances and never learned how to overcome it.

He was very skilled at returning shoplifted items and persuading the cashier to give him a refund absent of any receipt. One time he mistakenly tried to get a refund on an item he'd lifted at a different store. This led to a forced vacation at an Iron Bar Hotel. He had several vacations at several Iron Bar Hotels. Some judges aren't too lenient with those who have extensive records. He was an open book to this barber about his past mistakes. Several years ago he had asked for my confidentiality as long as he was alive. His stories about his escapades were hilarious.

My favorite Big D story started back in 2003. He hit me up for a $68 loan. He said he needed money for his prescription. I've always guarded against loaning money to anyone except my brother. I made an exception for Big D. I truly believed he would use the loan for drugs. I had my doubts as to whether or not he needed a prescription for the kind he was getting.

He made three installments within a few weeks. He got the balance down to $42. One $2 installment came in the form of a Butte County check dated in '03. I learned if you have cash in the pocket when arrested, it's documented. When released you don't get your cash back. The county issues a check. I never did deposit it. I liked to show others, I had loaned him money and sometimes he actually did make an effort to pay back.

Several months passed. No other payments were ever made. He quit coming to my shop. When I saw him elsewhere, I only said hello, never mentioning the money he still owed me. After five years had passed, I answered the phone at the shop one day. It was Big D. He asked, "I promise you when I get out, you'll be the first one I'll pay back. Can you send me a hundred to Susanville Prison?" I answered, "No, Big D, you've owed me $42 for five years, I'm not sending you any more."

Another five years passed. I had seen him at the store a couple of times after he was released and never mentioned the money he owed me. In 2013 Big D stopped in and told me, "I'm getting my check next week. It's been a long time, so I want to give you a hundred for what I owe you." I said, "No Big D, all I want is the $42 you owe me."

Sure enough, he shows up with the $42. He asked for a signed receipt. I ask, "What's this all about Big D?" He 'fessed up. He said he'd violated parole. He was out of town, stopped at a gas station and ate at their fast food joint and got a bad stomach. He wanted some over the counter medicine, but didn't have the $2.43 to buy a small bottle, so he shoplifted.

It didn't take a Sherlock Holmes to crack this case. The videos inside the store and on his license plate supplied enough evidence to land him in the County Jail.

When he got back home to Butte County he had to go to court for parole violation. The judge sentenced him to five years. When he visited the Home Arrest Officer for an interview, he had no idea the officer was one of my clients. When the officer got his hair cut we discussed stories about the customers we had in common.

The officer asked Big D, "Do you know Steve the Barber?" Big D said he answered, "Uh, buh, duh, yeah I do." … "Do you owe him any money?" Same answer, "Uh, buh, duh, yeah I do … If you pay him back I'll recommend you for home arrest." Big D liked the idea of staying home with a GPS ankle monitor rather than going back to prison. *THAT'S* why I got to collect the debt. Big D became a customer again for the rest of his days. He apologized many times for stiffing me and staying away for so long. He appreciated my friendship. He asked if he could have the ten year old two dollar, County Check back. I gave it to him and didn't even ask him for the two bucks. That is one of my favorite stories. It would take several books to tell all of the good ones.

One more good one … A man with a kid comes in the shop. The man gets his haircut first. When he's done, he said he wanted to go do something for a few minutes while the kid got his haircut. After the kid was done quite a while, I asked him if he thought his Dad was OK. The kid said he wasn't his Dad. He said that was just some guy who asked him if he wanted a free haircut.

Back to my Barber College days… I was seventeen, just out of high school. Besides shaving, cutting hair, sanitization and other necessary instruction, one of our teachers gave valuable advice on talking to, and especially, listening to, your customers. An important factor in building a clientele is conversation. He also hammered home the benefits of paying attention to the news. That was what many customers liked to talk about. Back then, news was on TV for only one hour a day. I had never seen a minute of it. My folks had no TV.

While attending Barber College, the boarding house I lived in had TV. I tried to watch the news. I thought it was boring. Unlike today, newscasters limited themselves to reporting only what had happened. They didn't offer up biased opinions. The '60 election was coming up. I never could figure out who any of the news people were going to vote for.

The instructor taught us the quickest way to build up a clientele was to listen, and agree with the customer. He said a lot of barbers like to spew their opinions and they think they are really smart. He said the real reason customers keep saying, "Right barber, right again barber" is because they don't want to get sideways with someone who has sharp tools in his hands.

Most of the rest of this book is based on actions and historical events involving Oroville City Government. Opinions of the author are based on observations and occurrences. The author was not privy to closed door sessions. Probably, a few times, the secret agreements which were not intended for public consumption were accidentally leaked within earshot of the barber chair.

My goal is for this book to be informative as well as entertaining. Texts which document history and quote legal codes and include bibliographic references can be dull and boring.

The title of this book, **Municipal Larceny vs Steve the Barber** suggests there were some legal violations. Larceny, as defined by Webster... *the illegal taking and removal of another's personal property without his knowledge or consent and with the express intention of depriving the owner of such property.* Municipal is defined as... *of, relating to or carried on by local self-government.* Municipal Larceny is a serious accusation.

Those of us uneducated in law find most legal text very difficult to understand. After struggling way too many hours attempting to get a grasp on legal lingo, I'm of the opinion that lawyers should be prohibited from becoming legislators. It looks like a conflict of interest to me. They can write confusing laws and then get hired to argue about them in court.

I feel it is necessary to quote five requirements from the California State Constitution. It was refreshing to read Article XIII D § 6. It was very well written and fairly easy for me to understand. It seemed to me the City of Oroville did not comply, or did not plan to comply, with the following five.

XIII D § 6(1) *The agency shall provide written notice, by mail, to each parcel (must include amount of fee, basis on which proposed fee was calculated, reason for the fee, and date, time, and location of a public hearing).*

XIII D § 6(2) *The agency shall conduct a public hearing within 45 days of mailing. If a majority of owners present written protests, the agency shall not impose the fee.*

XIII D § 6(2)(b)(1) *Revenues derived shall not exceed the funds required to provide the service.*

XIII D § 6(2)(b)(2) *Revenues derived shall not be used for any purpose other than for which the fee was imposed.*

XIII D § 6(2)(c) *No fee shall be imposed or increased unless and until that fee is submitted and approved by a majority of property owners subject to the fee, or at the option of the agency, a two-thirds vote of the electorate.*

My letters to the city regarding these overlooked requirements were never responded to.

CHAPTER THREE

Battle One: Industrial Recruiter

This chapter is the first of seven in a series which deals mainly with city government shenanigans. The goal of the author is to present his memoirs as if telling a story. Parts of these stories came from things that happened at city council meetings, other parts from barber shop conversations. When the author quotes words of others, as he remembers, it does not necessarily mean he shares their opinions.

Back around 1989 I appeared at an Oroville City Council meeting to speak about an issue of which I was concerned. I had picked the brains of some of my customers who were knowledgeable about such things. I took their advice and appeared in person rather than sending a letter.

It was a learning experience for me. Meetings have pre-printed agendas. Private citizens are allowed to speak on agenda items only during the discussion period allowed for each particular item. I was there to speak on a non-agenda item. If one wanted to speak on a non-agenda item, he or she, had to wait until the end of the meeting. At the beginning of the meeting I had no interest in city business and anticipated sitting through a long boring meeting until my turn came to speak. My disinterest would be ending soon.

Oroville, like most cities, welcomed businesses which provided jobs for the locals. An Industrial Recruiter had landed a six figure contract to attract businesses to Oroville. For the rest of the story, I'll refer to the Industrial Recruiter as 'SHE'.

SHE had a reputation of being very successful in recruitment efforts. SHE is credited for bringing many good jobs to Oroville.

Getting back to my first council meeting, I was sitting there thinking about what I was going to say instead of paying attention. SHE was at the podium when the conservative council member asked her a question. Her answer, "I'm not going to tell you" shocked me as well as some other attendees. There were some gasps. I surmised SHE and the conservative councilor must have locked horns before. Those words, "I'm not going to tell you" sounded like a battle cry to me. I never would have believed a contractor could get away with refusing to answer a question. I was one outraged taxpayer. I developed a sudden keen interest in Oroville politics. I decided I would be attending more meetings.

Like so many things in government of all levels, many details are confidential and not available to the general public. Thirty years got by before I contacted her in hopes of getting some more details for this chapter. SHE graciously responded to my request. SHE had vivid memories of her, "I'm not going to tell you" comment. SHE explained some businesses did not want recruiters to share information, so, confidentiality was part of the contract. I appreciated her filling me in. I explained to her, my complaint was with the mayor, not with her.

Back then, SHE enjoyed full support from the Mayor. For the rest of the story I will call him 'MAYOR.' MAYOR was a generation older than me. He retired from a career in education, first as a teacher, and then on to administration. He became a Principal, and if memory serves, finished up as a Superintendent. I knew him since I was in grammar school. He had been a customer in each of the five barbershops I worked at in town.

I remember very well, MAYOR once said during a council meeting, "SHE is the best thing that ever happened to Oroville. I'll vote for anything SHE wants." I didn't like that. I could see the flood-gates opening from the city coffers to her purse.

MAYOR, during one of his council meeting accolades, stated, SHE was responsible for bringing the recent expansion of the local cannery, a food processing plant, PCP, to town. He supported her claimed accomplishment by saying, "They could have gone to Lodi." The next day I called the corporate headquarters in Lodi, a town a couple hours south of Oroville. I told the person in charge I was doing some research on Oroville's Industrial Recruiter for a story in the local newspaper. He gave permission to use his name. I asked if SHE was responsible for PCP's decision to do the expansion in Oroville. He said there was no choice. PCP's only other property was in Lodi and there was no room for expansion. It was Oroville or not at all. My letter to the editor quoted everything he had said.

I couldn't wait for the next council meeting. I expected some gratitude for doing some leg work and revealing the facts. This didn't happen. The plant manager of Oroville's PCP spoke at the next council meeting. He had nothing but words of praise for what SHE had done to expedite things along the way. He thanked her for cutting through the red tape. I was getting a little confused.

I hadn't bothered to read the agenda before the meeting. Coincidentally, PCP was on the agenda toward the end. They had requested to lease three-fourths of an acre of city property across the street from the plant for a parking lot. At the end of the meeting, the City agreed to the lease for one dollar a year. I didn't like being blindsided. This taught me something else.

Always read the agenda prior to attending a meeting. I had no problem with the city giving a sweetheart deal to a company who provides jobs. I still don't. I suspected MAYOR might have put some pressure on the Plant Manager in order to shine a positive light on his Golden Girl. Now, SHE would not have to retract her claim of a successful recruitment.

Several years went by before Linda Tripp revealed the evidence of the Blue Dress which forced the sitting President to change his story and own up to one of his transgressions. I'm sure Tripp felt, when the irrefutable evidence, she was responsible for, was made public, the entire country would be grateful for the exposure of some presidential untruthfulness. It turned out, neither her efforts on a national scale, nor mine on a local scale, was appreciated enough to influence anyone.

The conservative council member made some of the following comments at the barber shop and others at council meetings.

If I remember correctly, he stated, the amount SHE received as add-on compensation for winning California's designation of Enterprise Zone was $26,000. The City Staff had prepared an application for the Enterprise Zone several years earlier which was not approved. He claimed SHE hired a college student, a Chico State intern, for a few weeks at six dollars an hour to update the City's application. Included in the application was a map defining the boundary of the Enterprise Zone. SHE must have had some influence in the California Legislature because this time approval was expedited. An Enterprise Zone gives some state tax relief to businesses who open up or expand within the boundaries.

I do remember, it was at a council meeting, when the conservative councilor took exception to $26,000 being spent on such a fast deal. SHE responded, "What are you complaining about? It's a win/win/win. You got what you want, I got what I want, and an intern got a job!" My take was, MAYOR's Golden Girl was growing some tarnish, whether MAYOR could see it or not.

The conservative councilor was not done. Later he accused her of violating the *Oroville Exclusive* clause of her contract. He claimed SHE had recruited a business for the city of Crockett, a couple of hours away from Oroville. SHE informed me there was no exclusive clause and she never worked for the city of Crockett.

My guess is most of the council felt SHE should be dismissed. Her contract was not renewed.

I don't believe my concern about the legitimacy of a recruitment claim had any impact on the council's decision. However, the story of SHE did motivate me to pay closer attention to local politics.

The best part of the story, MAYOR and I remained friends and he was my customer for the rest of his years. During our barbershop conversations, the story of SHE never came up.

The Story of She and The Mayor
Wins the Bronze Medal

CHAPTER FOUR

Battle Two: Fire Inspection Fee

Fast forward to March of 2012. This battle went on for several months also. I opened a letter from the City of Oroville which announced a new fee had been established for the Fire Department inspections of Oroville's businesses. When I read the details, I became outraged.

The letter demanded I make a payment to the City in the amount of $53.50 to pay for a future fire inspection of my business. The hourly rate the City assigned to recover the cost of conducting fire inspections was $107. They estimated my business would take thirty minutes to inspect.

Ten years earlier, the Fire Department inspected my business. A full company of Firemen rolled in and parked in my lot. There were no sirens or flashing lights, but I went outside to look around for the smoke anyway. One Fireman headed my way while the others spread out in all directions to inspect the other businesses in the neighborhood.

My inspection was completed in less than two minutes. He looked at the tag on the fire extinguisher to make sure it was not out of date, he checked the breaker box in the utility closet to verify it was labeled correctly, and might have glanced around the water heater in case there was gasoline or dynamite close to the pilot light. I signed the inspection form and he was gone. It took less than two minutes. There was no fee back then.

Now, when there is an hourly fee, the same inspection will take thirty minutes? It looked to me like a money grab. I decided to do battle with City Hall.

The first order of business was to study the law. California has a *Health and Safety Code*, a *Code of Regulations*, a *Fire Code*, as well as a *State Constitution*. Before the next City Council meeting I felt I needed to spend many hours researching.

Understanding legal text did not always come easy. Some things I had to read fifteen to twenty times to make sure I got it right.

I also spent a lot of time rounding up a bunch of other business owners to show up at the next City Council meeting. I figured an army of protestors would have more influence than going in solo. Twenty-six of us showed up for the next meeting of April 3, 2012. Seven of us took the podium to voice our objections. The battle was under way.

Before the meeting even started, I believe I spotted a legal violation printed right in the agenda. In the Staff Report under 'Fiscal Impact' was printed the words 'General Fund Revenue.' Regarding revenue derived from *Fees*, the California Constitution states *"Revenues derived shall not be used for any purpose other than for which the fee was imposed."* General Fund dollars are available to be spent on whatever the majority of City Council wants.

The City Administrator orally verified the city's intent of using the revenue for other purposes by stating, "If these charges are not enforced, the employees will still be there for this year. At some point in time, when the city does not have enough money, either those employees won't be there, or Parks Department employees won't be there, or the museum will be shut down, or something."

This statement established intent to violate another California Constitutional requirement, *"Revenues derived shall not exceed the funds required to provide the service."* It was clear to me, if the City of Oroville had chosen to be legally compliant there would be no extra revenue for employees or museums. The legal amount of revenue cities were allowed to collect could not exceed the *actual cost* of performing the service.

I had also boned up on the notification requirements for cities who wanted to impose new taxes or fees or raise existing taxes or fees. Oroville had only ran a newspaper notice which appeared on December 24, 2011. They did not bother to notify each parcel, by mail, as required by the California Constitution.

At the council meeting on April 3, 2012, when I was invited to speak at the podium, I did not know that if an on duty fireman conducted an inspection at a business, the City had the option to charge that business for the time the fireman spent performing his task. My logic told me if the fireman was responding to an emergency, conducting an inspection, washing a fire truck, working out in the gym, or relaxing in the city hammock while on duty, his pay was exactly the same. To me, the *actual cost* of conducting the inspection would be for travel expenses and inspection report forms. The fee money derived for the fireman's time spent does not go to the fireman, it is extra money for the city. I called it **Municipal Larceny.**

During the council's discussion, one councilor stated there should not be a fee imposed for the first inspection. He mentioned he thought $53.50 to inspect Dutch Brothers drive through coffee, could not be justified. Another councilor responded … "They make that much in ten minutes." This bothered me. In my opinion, the speed at which the money hits the till does not justify the city grabbing some of it.

City Council Chambers are in no way level playing fields. Private citizens are given up to three minutes to speak. After my first three minutes, City Staff used twenty minutes for rebuttals. There is no clock on them. Occasionally a speaker will be invited to revisit the podium if a councilor or staff member has a question or two. A friend tried to get me more time. He spoke a few seconds and then said, "I yield the rest of my time to Steve Christensen." The City Attorney wouldn't hear of it. He responded, "This isn't the United States Congress, you can't yield time!" It was worth a try. Through the years, I have suffered through many three minute deliveries from private citizens whose silly concerns were every bit as boring as barstool inebriated blathering. Overall the three minute limit is a good idea.

Remembering back to the previous inspection from 2002, the inspectors went to ten other businesses while the truck sat in my lot. All eleven business inspections were completed in around a half hour. Had fees been in effect then, the city would have collected a total of $909.50 from the eleven of us.

This amount vastly exceeds recovery of *actual costs*. Back then it took $276 every hour of the year to fund the entire Fire Department. The $900 plus for a half hour was more than enough to take care of the entire city budget for an hour and twenty minutes. **Municipal Larceny** is a very appropriate definition.

During the course of the battle, my wife, Lorraine and I sent over thirty letters to the city. I think the tide began to swing our way when we discovered and revealed that Fire Chief Charles Hurley had failed to abide by the California State Fire Code when he hired a retired fireman for $15 an hour to conduct fire inspections. We were alerted by another barber shop owner who had just been inspected. The letter from the City said the inspections would only be conducted by current, qualified, Fire Department employees. We made some inquiring phone calls to the City and felt like they were reluctant to give us answers. I called it stonewalling. Those businesses, the retired guy inspected, were still charged the entire $107 hourly rate. To me, this certainly did not comply with the legal *recovery of cost* limitation.

We gained even more ammo when I shared a partial communication from a taxpayer friendly organization, Howard Jarvis Taxpayers Association, with the city. I redacted everything except ... *"We do not disagree with you that the City of Oroville may be violating the law."* Howard Jarvis was very helpful with several things. They advised me to study Article 13 of the California Constitution.

I had mentioned to the city council, during an earlier meeting, I had received some correspondence from Howard Jarvis. I think one councilor thought I was running a bluff. He asked me three times if I could provide a copy. After delivering copies to all councilors and Department Heads, I expected a thank-you. I didn't even charge the twenty-five cents per sheet the city charges me for requested copies. A thank-you, or even an acknowledgement of receipt, would have been acceptable. Neither ever came from anyone with the city, elected or hired.

As the battle raged on, fewer business owners showed up at council meetings to continue the effort. I think the general consensus has always been, all one can do is show up and let off a little steam. They really didn't think City Hall could ever lose. Several of us decided to stay the course.

At several meetings the city seemed to put a great deal of importance on the fact that provisions for them to charge fees had been on the books since 1983. I guess they figured this would make them exempt from the written notice requirement which they had ignored regarding this new fire inspection fee. Article 13 D of the California Constitution requires written notification for *existing*, *new* or *increased* fees. There were times I suspected I might be the only one who had read the law. Other times I thought the city just took a shortcut, hoping they wouldn't get called on it. Only a short amount of time had elapsed since the California Supreme Court had created owner notification requirements which allowed the opportunity for property owners to protest rate increases.

The City Attorney caught me completely off guard at one meeting. He presented another flimsy reason why Oroville should be allowed to squeak out of the notification requirements. After I got home I did some additional research of the California Constitution and came to realize I had been out-played. The City Attorney said the requirements did not apply because of the heading **Property**. I learned the 500 year old United Kingdom definition of property meant real estate only. The current definition of property is spelled out within the California Constitution. It is also written in 13 D… *"Property ownership shall be deemed to include tenancies of real property where tenants are directly liable to pay the assessment or charge in question…all fees or charges shall comply with this section."* Personal effects, furnishings, machinery, inventory, franchises, patents, other rights subject to ownership, among many, many other things are correctly defined as property in today's America. Had I known this during the meeting, I might not have been allowed to counter the City Attorney anyway, given I'd already burned my three minutes.

After the five month battle, the City Council agreed to amend the Fire Inspection Fee by a vote of six to one. The City classification my business happened to be in (B occupancy) would not have to pay the fee for the fire inspection. Any other City business classification would still be subject to the fee. The councilor who voted **NO** was the only one who got it right, in my opinion. Even though I had been the squeaky wheel who got the grease, I felt the exemption should apply to all businesses. When the votes came in and I realized you actually can beat City Hall, I yelled out, "I love America." The banner headline in the local newspaper the next day, August 8, 2012, featured our win. My "I love America" outburst got some ink. Even though the victory had been earned through a long, hard battle, the whole story was not quite over yet.

I was curious why the City Attorney did not advise the council to repeal the decision to impose the fee months earlier. We got along very well during the dispute. We had some personal visits, phone calls, and e-mail correspondence. There was even some joking and laughing. He had mentioned early during our skirmish sometimes people filed suit when they challenged cities with legal violations. I think he had me pegged. He could tell I was not the type to say, *I don't care how much it costs, right is right, and wrong is wrong.* I've heard there are some who are willing to spend thousands of dollars to protect fifty. Believe me, I'm not one of those.

To me, some of the legal text in the California Constitution was so well written, even those of us who had not studied law found it easy to understand. Even though the battle was behind us, I was still curious why it took so long.

I thought it was possible the City Attorney received additional pay if he had to litigate in court. I requested a copy of his contract. Usually requested copies are not available immediately. You get a phone call after they are ready. You go to City Hall and pay your twenty-five cents per sheet and pick them up. I was very surprised when the City Attorney showed up, in person, at my shop to deliver the copy of his contract. He collected five dollars for the package.

I told him I thought maybe things were slow in the lawyer business. Maybe he wanted to bill the city for some more hours. Maybe he hoped I'd file a lawsuit so he could pick up a little extra cash. He said that wasn't it, he had plenty to do. As he was leaving, I told him it was a good thing, for him, we didn't have to go to court, as it would have looked bad on his résumé if he lost to a barber.

The Fire Department never did conduct another inspection of my business after the one in 2002. Starting in 2012, I received quarterly billings for $53.50 for a fire inspection for almost two years. I hand delivered the billing of January 1, 2013, to the City Attorney at a council meeting. I mentioned the fee had been reversed for five months.

I asked why the city kept sending me billings. Other business owners had the same concern. His letter of explanation arrived a few days later.

Since the fee reversal did not go into effect until October 6, 2012, all inspections prior to that date were still subject to the fee. His letter, in part … *The City Council did not and cannot retroactively change fees charged for services rendered by City personnel. In researching this matter further it appears that an investigation was not conducted of your business in 2012. Accordingly the City will reverse the billing for 2012 for your business.* Guess what? The billings kept showing up every three months.

My last letter to the City of Oroville pertaining to the fire inspection fee was delivered almost a year and a half after I was told of the fee reversal. It was dated May 19, 2014. I'll recreate it.

Oroville City Council/Staff   **5/19/14**

I was very happy on August 7, 2012, when Oroville City Council reversed its decision to impose fire inspection fees on "B Occupancy" businesses. My business is a "B Occupancy" business.

Since that date I have received seven quarterly statements requesting payment for a fire inspection.

I would like to know why.

Is it because there are some budgetary advantages to include some phantom entries under Accounts Receivable? You could do that without wasting valuable taxpayers money on postage.

Is it because some business owners will pay up whether the fee is valid or not? If one pays, it'll cover the cost of fifty mailings.

Is it because you enjoy my letters so much you knew I'd eventually write one if you continued to bill me?

I'd really like to know why.

Sincerely, Steve Christensen

Mayor Linda Dahlmeier, who I blasted several times before and since, called me and told me how much she enjoyed the letter. Regardless of the blastings, we are pretty good friends. Every-time we see each other she gives Lorraine and me a hug.

I have the distinction of being the first speaker she ever gaveled down at a council meeting. Things like this should never interfere with friendship. I still voted for her.

Once, after a council meeting ended, Lorraine and I were chatting with the City Attorney. Mayor Dahlmeirer came over and suggested we should all go have a glass of wine and discuss things. Then she asked, "Do you drink?" I got a good one in. I said, "Only after these meetings."

Several times Dahlmeirer and I were of opposite opinions. She felt the city's financial woes were a result of insufficient revenue, which could only be remedied by raising taxes. I felt if the city refrained from wasteful spending there would be plenty of money to take care of all essentials, plus some extra for Pie in the Sky.

At one council meeting, she invited some local charities to apply for some of the city's surplus funds. This annoyed me. I was present to protest the city's effort to establish the new fire inspection fee on businesses. I thought, "Why are they squeezing me for more when they have money to give away?"

A couple of my critical letters to the editor had appeared in the paper. Letters of similar content had been delivered to the city council and staff. One day, I was very surprised to see her walking toward my shop after parking her car. That visit led to our friendship. After a very pleasant conversation, she barely got out the door before I phoned Lorraine and said, "You'll never guess who came by to visit."

In the meantime the city had dismissed the Finance Director. She had been a city employee for many years and had worked her way up through the ranks. There was some litigation. Rumor has it she prevailed and won a settlement. The city then hired a very capable Interim Finance Director. He discovered some flaws, made some changes which benefitted the city coffers more than enough to cover his compensation for the whole time he worked for the city.

The Interim Finance Director graciously responded to the last letter and the billings finally ceased. It was refreshing to know we finally had somebody who knew how to stop invalid billings from showing up in the mail. He'd only been on the job a few months. He became my customer for the rest of the time he worked for the city. I learned a lot about city business from him every time he got a haircut.

The Fire Inspection Fee is Awarded
the Silver Medal

CHAPTER FIVE

Headscratchers & Boondoggles

Many Flavors of Squandering

1) First ... the Worst

In California, Grand Juries are required to investigate and provide written reports on government agencies within their counties. In 2018 Butte County's Grand Jury titled their report on the City of Oroville, Oroville: A City In Turmoil. Within the report the words, disarray, distrust, accusations of illegal behavior, etc., reflected an unfavorable view. Since very few people read the Grand Jury Report, I decided to send a letter to the editor so more voters would be aware of their findings. The name of California's public employee retirement program is CalPERS. The editor printed some of the text from the Grand Jury Report which I sent in. In essence it said the cost of withdrawing from CalPERS was prohibitive. To alleviate the situation in 2016, Oroville City Council put a local measure (Measure R) on the ballot to temporarily increase the sales tax by one percent.

A few days after the letter appeared, the city council had a daytime Budget Workshop scheduled. It was the afternoon of April 25, 2018. A friend called me at my shop. He was watching the meeting and alerted me my name was mentioned. The next day or two, I went to City Hall and bought a video of the meeting for five dollars.

During the meeting, Mayor Dahlmeirer said she had read my letter and disagreed with some things. She saw I was the one who had written it and proceeded to blame me for the words of the Grand Jury. She said what I wrote was not true.

I delivered a letter to the city the next day. I informed them the Grand Jury did not interview me nor commission me to write their report. I told them if anyone has a problem with the Grand Jury's findings, accuse them, not me. I suppose it's possible the Grand Jury was mistaken. I really don't know. All I did was send in a few of their words to the editor hoping he would print it so more people would be aware of their findings. My letter to the city never was responded to. Sometimes council members retract their mis-statements. I don't know if a retraction was ever made in this case.

The 2017-18 city council was not cohesive. Most controversial issues were decided by a vote of five to two. The two members who had experienced life in the private sector, Mayor Linda Dahlmeier and Scott Thomson usually voted opposite of those with public sector careers.

According to the City Charter, before being seated, those elected to serve must swear to an oath of office. They are bound to … **uphold the Constitution of the United States and the constitution of the state and carry out impartially the laws of the nation, the state and the city and thus to foster respect for all government.**

The first time I was aware the five violated the oath happened at the council meeting on February 20, 2018. Local legalization of cannabis was on the agenda. Doug LaMalfa, United States Congressman from our district, spoke to the council at that meeting. He warned them the nine federally funded programs and projects in our district would be at risk if they chose to ignore the federal position on cannabis.

As usual, the vote was five to two. From that day on, the five councilors were affectionally known as the "Marijuana Five."

Their next violation of the oath of office happened on July 10, 2018. This time it was a state law which was violated. It is called the **Brown Act**. The Brown Act mandates requirements and limitations for California's legislative bodies. Immediately after ignoring legal advice from the City Attorney, the Marijuana Five voted to censure Mayor Dahlmeier by a vote of five to zero. Dahlmeier and Thomson were absent. The council then had to schedule a special meeting a few days later and repeal the illegal action. I guess they finally decided they should heed the advice of those schooled in law. The state of California is very forgiving to the elected who ignore legal guidelines while legislating. Usually, all that needs to be done is to reconvene and perform a *cure and correct.*

A following violation of the Brown Act led to a visit from Butte County District Attorney. It was a short time before election day. He warned the five there is a saying, don't get a third strike.

He said if they did he would charge them with misdemeanors. Two of the MJ5 were defiant instead of grateful for being let off the hook twice. Jack Berry blurted out, "Arrest me." Marlene DelRosario was caught on a hot mic, after the meeting, telling the DA "That was an a**hole thing to do. You're just trying to impress your drinking buddies."

Their defiance may have turned out to be a blessing for the city. It could have cost both of them some votes. They were both seeking to be re-elected. They both lost. The MJ5 lost control. The remaining MJ3 were soon to be in the voting minority.

Mayor Dahlmeier did not seek re-election. It must have been a bitter pill for the MJ3 to swallow when new-comer Chuck Reynolds replaced Dahlmeier as mayor with two-thirds of the votes. Vice Mayor, Janet Goodson, one of the original MJ5, was his opponent.

The ugliest chapter in the history of Oroville City government was about to begin. After two years of domination by the MJ5, they seemed unable to respect the voters' decision to put a new captain in charge.

Late in December of 2018, before Reynolds was even sworn in, two councilors, Janet Goodson, and Linda Draper informed him, as to which committees they would be willing to serve on and which ones they would rather not be on. The mayor is charged with appointing committee members. He had different ideas on who he wanted serving on which committees. He did not allow them to cherry pick. So, taking them at their word, and not wanting to force anyone to serve on committees they didn't like, he made the decision to remove them from all committee assignments.

It didn't take long for the two to lawyer up and file a suit against the people of Oroville. Their law firm, Olson, Hagel, and Fishburn LLP, sent a letter to the city suggesting discrimination on three fronts, sexism, racism, and political party affiliation. The City Administrator estimated the cost to the city could approach $500,000, should the two prevail in court.

Potential litigation is only discussed in closed door sessions. I understand when the plaintiffs are council members they would not be allowed to attend sessions when their case was being discussed. Before the two decided to drop the flimsy lawsuit, $86,000 had been wasted preparing for litigation. $40,000 went to an out of town legal firm for an unbiased opinion and $46,000 worth of man-hours were burned by our City Attorney. The two were reinstated as committee representatives when the mayor re-assigned them to committee seats. Even though they did not get on their requested committees, they dropped the charges.

The two had won their seats in the 2016 election. Shortly after the election, I e-mailed our City attorney and apologized for the mistake of the voters. They had picked the people he would soon have to deal with. I wanted him to know I hadn't voted for either one.

2) Disappearing Keys

After the 2018 election, the two lame duck councilors Jack Berry and Marlene DelRosario had three meetings to attend before surrendering their seats.

After one of those meetings, the video showed DelRosario picking up a fob of keys and placing them in her purse before exiting.

A while later, Mayor Dahlmeier could not find her keys. Again, no Sherlock Holmes was needed to crack this case. Charges were filed. DelRosario denied the charges.

I was happy Mayor Dahlmeier refused to make an out of court settlement. I even phoned her and thanked her. I guess a common tactic is to delay and postpone court hearings as long as possible when a defendant is obviously guilty. This went on for a whole year. When the opportunity for delaying tactics had run its course, a plea of *nolo contendere* (a watered down version of guilty) ended the case.

3) Blanket Approval

Lack of fiscal discipline led the city into budgetary shortfalls. In 2017 essential services had to take some cuts. As strong as city employee unions had been, they agreed to 10% pay-cuts. The City Council at this time made a horrible blunder. After accepting the pay-cuts from the employees, they awarded themselves blanket approval to attend seminars and conferences for a whole year. Before this action, each trip had to be considered and voted on by council. Now, none of these opportunities for free junkets could be denied.

There were eleven categories of conferences and seminars. Some of these had multiple events spread all across the country. Some were yet to be scheduled and costs were unknown. Every week or two an event would be happening somewhere. Blanket approval gave them the option to attend the most distant and costly ones if they chose. City employee morale sank to its lowest level ever. The city had cried "poor." So, the employees all took a hit, and now councilors voted to have more money for themselves to travel on. This didn't go over too well.

Blanket approval was on the agenda for 10/3/17. The headline which was in the local newspaper one week earlier was "Pensions Could Bankrupt Oroville." Both Lindas on Oroville City Council, Mayor Linda Dahlmeier and councilor Linda Draper, tried to sell us on the notion that blanket approval was a money saver. They deceptively implied there could be savings by lumping a whole years worth of conferences and seminars together and funding them all at once.

These two took turns stating that staff reports take up to $1,500 worth of man-hours for staff to prepare. They made it sound like costs to the city could rise as much as $1,500 each time a staff report was requested. That's deception. The cost is arrived at by reverse engineering. If a clerk spends ten hours on a project, they use the pay scale of the clerk and attach the cost of labor accordingly. They add some more costs in, maybe some for the time the City Attorney reviews it, for some fixed costs, office footage, a percent of utilities, etc., and arrive at a figure. If the clerk was asleep in the office for the same ten hours, the costs would be exactly the same. City employees are paid by the hour, not by their volume of production. It seems to me, the only way a city could save any money would be if the work-load is reduced sufficiently to justify eliminating a position.

There is another very good reason I was so dead set against blanket approval. A year or so earlier the Acting City Administrator requested funding to attend a conference in Denver, Colorado. He didn't like planes and wanted to take a train. That would add a day each way for travel. When lodging and per diem costs were tallied up, the cost of the trip would amount to several thousand dollars on top of the gate fee.

When someone pointed out the same conference was scheduled for nearby Sacramento, the only extra money he got was for round trip mileage reimbursement. He looked like someone hit him on the toe with a hammer. Had blanket approval been in effect back then, he'd have gone to Denver on a whole bunch of our dimes.

On October 15, 20, and 25, of 2017, councilor Draper and I had a little sparring match with letters to the editor which were printed in the local newspaper. The best letter to the editor was printed exactly one month after the council meeting.

> **Tim A Duzmal wrote,** *The great Abraham Lincoln once cautioned the politicians. You can fool all of the people some of the time, you can fool some of the people all of the time, but you cannot fool all of the people all of the time. Those who sit on Oroville City Council have little hope for a future in politics. As hard as they try, they can't even fool Steve the Barber.* **I rate this as the best letter to the editor of all time.**

4) Jamboree Housing

Two months after the Blanket Approval fiasco, the Jamboree Housing project (low income) was on the agenda. There was sure to be some resistance from the public on this. If you had to pick which of these two issues, Blanket Approval or Jamboree Housing undermined the public's trust to the greatest extent, Jamboree Housing would have to come out on top.

The Staff Report on the item included a request for a deferment of fees for the housing development. The devil was in the details. The amount of the requested fee waiver totaled over $816,000. The language within the request would allow Jamboree to defer any payments for the entire duration of the term of the note, fifty-five years. This is worth repeating, Fifty-Five Years. I hand delivered a letter of concern to City Hall the morning of the meeting. Two hours before the meeting was scheduled to begin, the decision was made to table this one item for two weeks until the next scheduled meeting. Lorraine and I attended. We witnessed a horrible breach of the public trust.

During the discussion, some concerned citizens voiced opposition to more low-income housing for Oroville. The Housing Needs Authority data for our area reflected a great need for above average housing, not low cost housing. The council's spokesperson was Linda Draper. She said Jamboree's unit mix called for 44% of the units to be for above average income tenants. I thought she had some knowledge of some details which had not been made public. When I was at the podium, I asked Draper where she got this information. She said page two of the Staff Report. I said I would have to read it again. Page two did not confirm her statement. A month later, she did make a retraction. A completely different reason was given for the *mistake*. I do not know if it was a mistake or not. There is the possibility she was trying to deceive.

I wrote several letters and e-mails to the city seeking information. The most beautiful e-mail I ever received arrived January 4, 2018. It was the unit mix from Jamboree. It stated in part, "Mr. Christensen is correct ... 100% of units are set aside for Low income households or below."

Motivated to share this information with as many who would listen, I sent a letter to the editor which appeared January 11, 2018. Under the heading of Erosion of Trust Follows Oroville Council Discussion, was printed, in part, *Oroville City Council has a new problem. A serious mistake made by the council Dec. 19 slipped under the radar. During the council's discussion on Jamboree Housing, Council Member Linda Draper said 44% of Jamboree's units were reserved for tenants of above moderate income. Since no one from the council or staff challenged this statement, I imagined the city was in agreement with her based on some details which had not been made public.* The letter ended with, *If others from the council or staff were unaware of this unit breakdown, that raises concern about their competence. If some were aware and still remained silent after Draper's false statement, their integrity should be questioned. All people of Oroville's public sector, unaware of the facts, or deceitfully silent, are responsible for the erosion of the public's trust on this one.*

Acting City Administrator, Don Rust, immediately after the first meeting in February was over, admitted to me, he knowingly allowed the misstatement to stand uncorrected. I asked him why. His answer triggered another letter to the editor which was printed February 11, 2018. He explained, **I didn't want to embarrass anybody**. I was outraged. I believe sparing embarrassment is not a valid reason to give councilors the green light to stray from truthfulness.

Contracted Department Heads are given a severance settlement when dismissed by a vote of council. It's my understanding, if they resign, there is no severance settlement. Nine days after my letter appeared, Mr. Rust gave notice he was moving on. I couldn't help but wonder if he was trying to get fired when he admitted to allowing falsehoods to stand. If he had pulled that off, he might have laughed his head off all the way to the new job.

The Grand Jury's assessment of **Oroville: A City in Turmoil** will continue to gain credence throughout the rest of this chapter and some of the following chapters.

When citizens are aware the city has chosen to squander its way to a budget crisis, voter approval of tax increases becomes very difficult. Some of us feel we have good reason to not trust our city government with more revenue just because the city cries *poor*.

5) Gateway Project

The City spent at least $1,380,000 on real estate and expenses for a 20 acre project named Gateway. Eight years later council voted to sell it to a developer for one dollar. Luckily, there was a buy-back clause in the event the developer failed to make infrastructure improvements on time. Another eight years have passed. No infrastructure projects have even been started, let alone completed. I do not know if we gave back the dollar and got the 20 acres back, or if we even collected the dollar in the first place.

6) Sewer Fund Raided Twice

Sewer tax increases are rubber stamped automatically every four or five years no matter how robust the Sewer Fund is. At the end of 2014, $875,000 was taken from the Sewer Fund to purchase 13 Public Safety vehicles. I learned it is legal as long as an IOU is thrown in with a payment schedule, including interest. A few years later, the Finance Director reported it had been discovered $800,000 existed in a restricted Sewer Fund account since 1997. She asked for the restriction to be lifted so the money could go to the General Fund. I guess they want to guard against an *overflowing* Sewer Fund.

7) Kayak Ditch

I was told $247,000 went for research on the feasibility of diverting water from the Feather River to feed a man-made Kayak Run. Some **Pie in the Sky** dreamers feared there were not enough restaurants or motel rooms to support the thousands of visitors who would be clogging the Highways and Byways trying to get here every day. This brought to mind the days I was a rookie barber and the over-enthusiastic optimists anticipated a full reservoir behind the dam under construction. They said by 1990 the population of Butte County would double, all of it here. Chico would become a bedroom community for Oroville. Mansions would adorn the hills overlooking the lake. Four traffic lanes would be needed to the campsites and boat launches. They were wrong. The first wave of visitors was sizable. However, they took home tales of rattlesnakes and poison oak and never returned. The Kayak Ditch idea eventually went down the drain and took the $247,000 with it.

8) Tire Crumbs

CalRecycle had a program which dealt with tire recycling. Old tires would be ground up into crumbs to be used for ground cover. Oroville mistakenly bought in, absent of sufficient research. The city accepted delivery of a load of tire crumbs for $35,000. The deal was, the $35,000 would be returned to the City after the tire crumbs were placed.

Some concerned citizens spoke in opposition after the tire crumbs had been delivered. They contained carcinogens. Some had steel wire barbs. Some schools had used them several years earlier. A teacher told me kindergarteners' mouths had to be checked after recess to see if they had substituted tire crumbs for chewing gum. The city decided not to use them.

The City Administrator was concerned about not getting our money back if we didn't follow through. There was some discussion of trying to sell them at half cost. I thought if CalRecycle gives them free, nobody's going to buy, even at the 50% discount. Several months passed before a friend who worked at the City Corporation Yard told me they were gone. This was all I could get out of him. I never did find out the details of their disposal.

9) Locking Manhole Covers

I attended a meeting which had an Agenda Item regarding purchasing some locking man-hole covers to prevent people from lifting the unlocked models. The Public Works Director was very much in favor of purchasing the necessary 135 units from an out-of-town supplier for over $600 apiece. A local metal fabricator had made a presentation offering to outfit existing man-hole covers with locking devices for less than half the cost. He offered to give the city five different prototypes at no cost. For some reason, the Public Works Director seemed to be very driven to persuade the council to, at least, purchase 68 units from the out-of-towners for $42,000, immediately. I think he overstated the urgency of the situation. They went for it. It made sense to me to get all 135 for less than $42,000, and keep our tax dollars in town. Months later, my friend from the corporation yard told me the units had been piled up in the warehouse, and there was no urgency to have them installed.

10) Arts, Culture and Entertainment (ACE)

After reading the City Budget and asking why Department Heads were so generously compensated, I was told this is the going rate for quality, capable people. Our city hired another out-of-town firm, to the tune of $92,000 to come up with some kind of plan which links the city properties together, such as, museums, auditoriums and the State Theater. The goal was to establish a mapped in area to be dedicated to arts, culture, and entertainment. The out-of-towners produced a twenty-nine acre map that bordered the Feather River and made sure the appropriate city properties were within the boundaries. This could have been easily accomplished by our highly paid, quality, capable staff. Many homeless camps exist on the banks of the river. I sent a letter alerting them, I didn't think arts, culture, and entertainment would blend very well in the habitat of the homeless.

11) Sewer Map Mistake

Back when Oroville employed a City Engineer, it was thought some sewer mapping was needed. I have no idea why the City Engineer could not do the job. An out-of-town engineering firm, Carollo Engineering was awarded $516,000 to do the work. I did ask why we have an engineer on staff and still needed to hire outsiders. That question was never answered. Someone did tell me, confidentially, it was later discovered, we already had the work completed.

Luckily the contract was voided in time, and another half a million wasn't wasted.

There are instances when either state or federal law requires cities to allocate funding for stuff that seems ridiculous and wasteful to everyone, those in city government as well as private citizens.

My concerns are only with the type of financial blunders which the council could have, and should have, voted down.

They Wonder Why Some of Us Oppose Higher Taxes

CHAPTER SIX

The Big-One,
Measure R

The day after the election in 2014 the local news reported the neighboring town of Paradise won voter approval for a sales tax increase. I told Lorraine, Oroville would try for this next. That very day I began to research. I strongly believed in one of my campaign statements ... *If all the voters attended the same council meetings I had, a tax increase wouldn't get a single vote from anyone in the private sector.* Less than four months after election day, at the first meeting in March of 2015, the council voted to go for the sales tax increase as soon as possible. By then I had done a lot of research. I presented a nine point plan which would guarantee passage. The whole thing depended on a compromise. If the City would be willing to repeal the Utility User Tax (UUT) in a simultaneous action, I would be on board and support the proposed sales tax raise.

The projected new revenue, *IF* Measure R passed, was $3,600,000 annually. The UUT tax, which would be repealed, would cost the City $1,600,000 annually. The net gain of two million represented around a 17% increase in annual City revenue. The beauty of the compromise was 75% to 80% of the retail sales within the City limits did not come from city residents. It came from County residents and transients. It would have been an easy sell to voters once they realized their overall city tax burden would be cut in half by trading one tax for another. It's rare, indeed, when a government agency can honestly reduce overall taxes for its citizens by half, and significantly increase its own revenue. My letter to the editor printed on April 16, 2016, opened with some number crunching which led into my favorite line ... **We all know repealing any tax sounds worse than fingernails on the blackboard to the elected.** I went on to suggest the sacrificing of a smaller tax may be the only way to persuade voters to go for a more lucrative tax increase. Reducing city tax burden by half and giving the city a nice income boost sure sounded like a no brainer to me. I thought everyone would like a win/win. I was wrong.

The City's original plan in March of 2015 was to have a special election as soon as possible. They wanted more money immediately. I wanted more time to campaign against the tax raise since they had turned the noses up and pointed the thumbs down at the win/win compromise. They lost me. I decided to be a Mister Nice Guy, no more. The cost of a special election was estimated to be around $60,000. I decided this was my best argument in an attempt to delay the issue until the next regular election twenty months later, in November of 2016. Since a special election would only gain them a few months, it didn't take long before the City decided to wait until the General Election. The Measure R issue was tabled for almost a year. I had bought some time.

Countless hours were spent researching. It takes me a lot longer to find stuff than those more familiar with computers and the like. I never have learned how to marry a spread sheet to a calculator. I had to do things the old fashioned way. I tallied up stuff with a pencil and tablet. There are advantages to doing things the old fashioned way. You need to remember how the procedure works. This is a better mental exercise. Results stick better in the mind, to boot.

The rural, agricultural counties in California are well below average in income and above average in unemployment. When the City of Oroville had 87 employees, the City Budget showed $8,600,000 went for compensation packages. This is just a whisker under $100,000 apiece. Oroville's median household income at the time was between $27,500 and $35,000. Two different sources had two different numbers.

Some of those households had more than one breadwinner. My letter to the editor printed on August 14, 2016, had a paragraph I was especially fond of … *Many in higher levels of government have been very critical of private sector income inequality. Oroville has its own brand of income inequality. City employees compensation packages average almost four times the median household income. That's our brand of income inequality.*

It took many, many hours to come up with an accurate, verified comparison between the cities in Butte County and the six other counties which adjoin us. Since the economic demographics are similar in our cluster of counties, I figured the different average city tax burdens in our area would be worth taking a look at.

The differences were actually astounding. Even without any increased sales tax, Oroville residents' tax burden already averaged twice as much as any of the other cities in our seven county cluster. Oroville was only one of five cities in the seven counties which imposed any form of add-on tax.

Ours is called a Utility User Tax (UUT). Back in the nineties, a grassroots effort was put forward in an effort to repeal the UUT. Other California cities which had imposed UUTs without voter approval had already repealed theirs. Since Oroville had a poverty rate and unemployment numbers around double the state averages, some tax relief seemed to be a reasonable request. The effort did not succeed.

The other four cities which had an add-on tax had only raised their sales tax. The highest was ½%. If Measure R passed Oroville would have the distinction of having the highest sales tax, a full 1% as well as the only one with a utility tax. I earlier mentioned, solely because of the UUT tax, Oroville people were already paying twice as much money as people of any of the other cities who were saddled with an add-on sales tax.

Mayor Dahlmeier disagreed with comparing Oroville only to neighboring similar cities. She said state wide comparisons would be more appropriate. I was already loaded for bear. Before I isolated our seven county cluster and shared those numbers, I had conducted a very productive study of the entire State of California. The state agency formerly known as the Board of Equalization (BOE) had an enormous data bank. It was difficult and time consuming for me to find what I wanted, but I did pick up some valuable information for my side of the argument.

I don't like reading a lot of boring statistics myself, so I decided to inform readers only of the most important ones. More than half of California's cities managed to get by with neither form of add-on tax. Their lists of **HEADSCRATCHERS & BOONDOGGLES** must be much shorter and far less impressive than ours.

I compared Oroville to California's 534 other cities, which were divided into over 1700 districts. Several of these districts had per capita incomes of six, seven, eight, and up to nine times as much as Oroville. Not many had lower incomes. This was why I thought comparing similar cities in our part of the state would provide more realistic information.

After countless hours of tedious number crunching, the results showed, if Measure R passed, Oroville, in the bottom 4% of income, would also be in the top 4% of the highest taxed. To me, this was, by far, the most important point the voters should be made aware of.

I decided to do what I could to get this information out. Flyers were printed and distributed to other small businesses. Most restaurants in town had a cork-board for flyers. I made sure they all had one of mine pinned to it. Lorraine and I met a retired gentleman by the name of August Lincoln who wanted to help spread the word. He had read a flyer somewhere and stopped by my shop to learn more. After his visit, he stood in front of grocery stores, handed out flyers and talked to people. The last few weeks before the election, we only had the team of three. Lorraine and I had total expenditures of $60. We bought a ream of paper for the printer, an ink jet, and a small can of red paint for a sign in front of the shop. We did not form an official *No on Measure R* committee.

There was a *Yes on Measure R* committee. Their donations came from City Employee Unions and individual city employees. Their expenditures exceeded ours around a hundred times, six thousand dollars. They had glossy mailers printed which showed up in the mail boxes of voters. They hosted events which served refreshments. Some of my very good friends supported the tax increase. This did nothing to hurt our friendships.

Just like four years earlier when we fought the Fire Inspection Fee, we sent many letters to the editor which showed up in the local newspaper. The last couple months before the election, the editor warned writers, only one political letter would be printed from each individual writer. I had a few friends who allowed me to write letters and use their signatures. Before I sent those in I made sure those who let me borrow their names were in agreement with the content.

I was happy with the editorial which ran three weeks before the election. The editor supported our side. He used some of the information I had uncovered while researching California's Board of Equalization. He pointed out if Oroville voters approved the sales tax, we'd be among only twenty cities in the state which had both a full 1% sales tax increase and a UUT. Both the editor and I had serious concerns of the old *bait and switch* might be in play. The words, *Public Safety*, seem to make voters more receptive to tax increases. It's been rumored, more money is promised during campaigning, for whatever purpose advertised, than actually gets there after the money rolls in.

Lorraine and I were invited to write both the **Argument Against Measure R**, and the **Rebuttal to Argument in Favor of Measure R** which appeared on the ballot. Mayor Dahlmeier's signature was among those which appeared on the arguments for the other side.

Throughout the year of campaigning, there were several forums organized so people could hear both sides of the issue. My good friend, Public Safety Director for the city, Bill LaGrone always made sure we knew about those events. He did the arguments of support and we did the arguments of opposition. His was the only other signature along with Mayor Dahlmierer which appeared on both the argument and rebuttal for *Yes on Measure R* which appeared on the ballot. We made a friendly wager on who pays for lunch after the votes were tallied. We later decided to press the bet up to a dinner out, with wives included.

The Public Safety Director is both Police Chief and Fire Chief. Because of budgetary problems Oroville had reduced the number of Department Heads from eight, down to three. Back when the council consisted of six retired government employees and only one private sector member, some of us felt the city might have been overstaffed and more than sufficiently compensated. To me, three

Department Heads seemed to get the job done just fine. When the current council was sworn in at the first meeting in January of 2019, *efficiency* moved up on the priority list.

Not all public sector councilors were cookie-cutter voters. They do seem to see things differently than people from the private sector. It's best to have a mixture. Most private sector people, especially business owners, bring in some ideas which make good business sense. It's beneficial when some of the councilors who retired after careers in the public sector get to see a different slant on things.

If we'd only had this blend of councilors in the past, there may have never been a need for increased taxes. Some of those costly Headscratchers & Boondoggles might have been laughed out of the room during closed door sessions. I mentioned earlier, Oroville was seeking to be among the highest 4% in California in municipal tax burden placed upon its citizens.

Again, more than half of California's cities had neither form of add-on tax. In Oroville, lack of management had been the problem, not lack of revenue. On election day most voters agreed with me. *NO* votes tallied 2,934, *YES* votes 2,250. We won with 57% to 43%. If all the voters had attended the same council meetings I had, the result would have been the same. The percentages would have had more disparity.

In my opinion, the $8 million which was blocked from going to the city coffers for the following two years was much better off left in the pockets of Oroville shoppers. We got a few phone calls from other business owners thanking us for our efforts.

THE MEASURE R BATTLE
WON THE GOLD MEDAL

CHAPTER SEVEN

City Wants A Rematch

Oroville decided to try for the sales tax increase again. It was on the ballot for the 2018 election. The name was changed to Measure U. This effort actually started the day after the 2016 election, when Measure R went down. The chairman of the YES ON R committee stopped by my shop to offer congratulations and asked if I would be on board if they kept the UUT, and tried for a ½% boost next time. I still thought it would be better to repeal the UUT and have the sales tax go up the full 1%. The projected revenue for the city would be almost the same either way.

Self interest was part of the reason. The factors had not changed. The utility tax gave the city an average of $100 per citizen. The 1% sales tax increase, based on cost per person would only average around $50 per citizen, per year. Again, most shoppers in Oroville lived outside of the city. They would be supplying most of the city's increased revenue through the higher sales tax. Again, voters are very receptive to something which would actually lower their own tax burden.

After they decided to try again, I formed a new battle plan. I started with some *I told you so* letters. I thought it would be easy to persuade them to not make the same mistake twice.

The three rookie councilors who won seats in the 2016 election had been sworn in for six months when I sent them each a copy of the same letter. I told them when the previous council decided to go for a second add-on tax (1% sales tax increase) they were given a sure fire road map on how to secure voter approval. All they had to do was repeal the first add-on tax, the Utility Users Tax (UUT). I went on to explain the city revenue would increase by 17% in the amount of $2 million annually while the city tax burden on citizens would be cut in half. I finished my letter with, "It'll work this time. It would have worked last time."

Councilors Linda Draper and Marlene DelRosario said they would not be supporting a repeal under any circumstances. During a council meeting, Draper even said, "We'd be complete idiots to give up the utility tax." They said they didn't see how trading one tax for another could possibly have any advantages. It seemed to me, they had no idea what a win/win was. Give me the opportunity to sacrifice $1.6 M in order to receive $3.6 M. I'd be on that like a pit bull on a pork chop.

This time the city decided to hire an out of town consultant to help win votes. The consultant, William Berry came to his first city council meeting seeking a contract. He saw me in attendance at the council meeting. He came over to chat after recognizing me. He had seen me on the local TV news channel which was aired before the meeting. The TV reporter had brought his camera into my shop earlier that day. They wanted to hear from both supporters and opponents of Oroville's second shot at the sales tax increase. The next day I sent the city a thank-you letter because the council made me happy when they denied the request to approve $18,000 for the consultant. At a later meeting they gave him more than double, a $40,000 contract. I was not happy after that.

I sent subsequent letters to the city and newspaper still trying to trade the UUT tax for the sales tax. I could tell from listening to discussions from both City Staff and City Council, compromising to secure the sure thing was beginning to seem highly unlikely. They decided they still wanted to go for the whole enchilada. Again I wrote the argument which went on the ballot opposing the tax measure. Lorraine wrote the argument against cannabis which was also on the ballot.

Since the text in Measure U almost mirrored the words of the defeated Measure R from two years earlier, I wrote my favorite line which appeared on the ballot, "The consultant could have earned $10,000 per word by simply stating ... Try Again, No Changes." After the consultant picked up his city check he went straight to the bank and cashed it. I bet he laughed his head off all the way home to Sacramento.

I believed Measure U would suffer the same fate as Measure R. I was already thinking about how I could gloat and send some more *I told you so* letters. Those dreams were squashed when the voters went for it this time. One must always look for a silver lining. A businessman, Chuck Reynolds, had been elected Mayor and another conservative minded quality candidate from the private sector, Eric Smith, won a seat. The texture of the council changed for the better.

Even though I lost the rematch, I don't regret the effort. I wonder what would have happened if I had put in ten times the effort like I had two years earlier. We'll never know.

After the murder of George Floyd, rioters were not satisfied when murder charges were filed. Some became criminal anarchists. They seized ownership of streets and neighborhoods in many cities across the nation. Arsonists destroyed buildings and vehicles. Demonstrators displaying banners demanding defunding of police appeared in these cities. Even signs that have the words DEFUND THE POLICE on them are protected by our Constitution. I found it unbelievable when some politicians seemed be influenced, and even agreed with such a notion. Some cities actually did cut law enforcement funding.

If the majority of our citizens buys into this, tactics will need to change. Campaigning for tax increases, and promising the new money would bolster police protection, will no longer work. The new campaign slogan might become, "If you give us more tax dollars, we guarantee, it won't go to police!"

Sorry, I don't get it.

CHAPTER EIGHT

Another Rematch?

Maybe the city's victory wasn't enough revenge. Do they smell blood? Is it possible they'll put forward another effort to bring back the Fire Inspection Fee? Back during the first Fire Inspection Fee skirmish, eight years ago, I discovered previously, in California, if government agencies named what they squeezed out of the taxpayers **fees**, they could impose them by legislative vote. If they named them **taxes** voters got to decide. Again, *Tax* revenue can be disposed of any way the legislative body chooses. This is why Oroville got in financial dire straits. They disposed. There had been too many costly mistakes. A higher priority went on *Pie in the Sky* fantasies then taking care of the nuts and bolts. *Fee* money isn't supposed to be disposed of at the whims of a majority of legislators. There are very narrow parameters limiting what the proceeds of fees could be used for. Amounts are legally limited to *recovery of cost*. This is a very workable and fair way to proceed, if all who are involved follow the rules.

Not everyone elected to a political position, believes keeping their word belongs at the top of the priority list.

The California Proposition 13 from 1978 ended the open season on home owners when it slowed down the ability to raise taxes on parcels of real estate. Some creative government agencies devised ways to alleviate their unquenchable thirst for more and more of the people's money. Since the imposing, or raising of fees, needed no voter approval, opportunity presented itself and was seized by the clever legislators. It got so out of hand the *Mitigation of Fees Act* was passed around 25 years ago. The taxpayers guardians, such as *Howard Jarvis Taxpayers Association*, supported setting up some legal hurdles and blockades in order to slow down the abuse. Legislative bodies looked for ways to circumvent them.

One city, Rancho Cucamonga, during a building surge, over charged developers to the tune of several millions of dollars. The courts were very lenient with this case of Municipal Larceny. The way I understood the ruling, there would be no restitution for the victims. The court directed fees to be reduced to less than costs, until the city could show documentation the books were balanced. My imagination tells me, some book cooking was probably implemented to get there.

I was happy for Oroville when Public Safety Director Bill Lagrone moved up to City Administrator. A couple of years ago the city hired the very capable Tom Lando, former long term City Manager of the neighboring city of Chico as Interim City Administrator. The City of Oroville gave Lagrone his third hat, Assistant

City Administrator. LaGrone was being groomed to become the next City Administrator. I was also happy the City picked the best mentor one could ever hope for in Lando.

Department Heads are hired at the discretion of the council. It takes five of the seven to approve a hiring. Lagrone had only four supporters. One of the cronies of the anti-Lagrone group (the MJ3) proudly proclaimed at City Hall one day, "I control the fifth vote." The LaGrone opponents were up against a date on the calendar. There was a deadline. They didn't know they were on the clock. When the clock ran out the Mayor was obligated to fill the position by appointment. He fulfilled his duty and LaGrone became our current City Administrator. LaGrone surrendered both his Police Chief and Fire Chief hats to a successor. It was rumored some of the out of town applicants for the job had been recruited by the LaGrone opponents. Tom Lando was not dismissed. He stayed on as Assistant City Administrator, a part time position.

In January of 2020 City Administrator LaGrone asked if I still had eight year old details from the Fire Inspection Fee skirmish. He hinted the idea was being discussed and the city might possibly try for it again.

I opened an old file box and brought out a stack of papers over a foot thick. I had kept the paper work on all my battles with City Hall in folders. I had newspaper clippings, letters to the editor and to the City Council and Staff in addition to some of my hand written notes. I looked through them and thought this stuff would make a good book. I cherry picked a few documents and made a package along with a cover letter for LaGrone.

Since LaGrone's only hat in 2012 said Police Chief on it, he might not have paid as close attention to a Fire Department issue back then. We had a Fire Chief in 2012, named Charles Hurley. My favorite Chief Hurley story came after he apologized to one of the brothers who owned Huntington's Sporting Goods Store. Besides a sizable retail operation in Oroville, they did world wide catalog sales. At the meeting before the apology, Huntington blasted Hurley. The Fire Department had conducted an inspection at his store. He said those inspectors were like ants at a picnic, all over the place. They would not stay out of restricted areas. Firearm retailers risk loss of federal license when restricted areas are breached. He was not happy and said so.

Two weeks later Hurley explained, along with his apology, during inspections, layouts of the building, door and window locations were being noted in case of a future emergency. If lighting wasn't available the Fire Department could be more effective if they knew the layout. My next letter had a little barb in it. I wrote...If I were a fireman, I'd quit my job before entering a burning ammunition store. I did not get a Christmas card from Hurley.

I don't know what is discussed behind closed doors in the Council Chambers. Everyone privy seems to respect the oath of confidentially. Some information they discuss is not secretive. I've been hoping to hear if they want to try for the fire fee again. Since they won the last sales tax bout, maybe they figure they got me softened up. Sometimes, I am not in the loop even when they are at liberty to share some of the information.

My highly visible business is the only small building located on a corner with a traffic signal. I am bordered, on two sides, by a large parking lot which belongs to the adjoining Shopping Center.

It's a perfect spot for political signs. I had displayed signs for several consecutive elections. Before the 2018 election I crossed paths with one of the councilors of the opposite persuasion. I asked her if she saw my sign, knowing that she was on the other side of every important issue. I got a kick out of her answer … "I avoid driving by *your* corner."

I'm hoping to hear from LaGrone. IF, the city does pursue the Fire Inspection Fee again, they better follow all the legal requirements this time. The issue well could have been put on hold. Like so many businesses in the private sector, city business has probably been delayed because of Covid 19. Those of us who oppose increased taxes will have the upper hand if everyone receives required written notification. When you get a letter from the city announcing a proposed tax or fee raise, you are truly notified. The newspaper notice printed back in 2011 had so little detail, if anyone read it, they would have had no idea what it was about.

If Oroville does bring back the Fire Inspection Fee, they'll be accused of attempting to set the California State record in highest municipal tax burden. I plan to be the accuser. I don't like the idea of Oroville going from the leading double dipper in the state to the biggest triple dipper.

CHAPTER NINE

City Keeps Illegally Collected Taxes

Somewhere around twenty years ago, the power company, PG&E, added Oroville's 5% add-on Utility Users Tax to billings of some customers which were not within Oroville City Limits. Ten or more years went by before the mistake would be corrected. Billings with the language *local tax* on them aren't specific enough to be questioned by county dwellers. If the billings said *Oroville City Tax*, maybe the mistake would have been noticed much earlier. When PG&E decided to inform the customers they were wrongly charged the tax, they sent written notices.

Since PG&E had forwarded the collected tax to the city, people were instructed to apply at City Hall for a refund. When the refunds came, the amounts only covered a refund of the most recent twelve months of the illegally charged taxes. The city claimed their decision to partially refund was legally compliant. Two home owners were outraged. They wanted to be refunded for the whole ten years. They sued in Small Claims Court and prevailed. Full refunds were issued, as far as I know, only to those two, which had sued. I asked the two if I could use their names in a letter to the editor, they preferred I didn't, so I've never told anyone their names.

At least one of the other victims was a business. It was one of two Indian Casinos which lie outside the City Limits of Oroville. Both tribes started with very small casinos and housing for tribal members. Both had expanded and now include hotels, showrooms, gas stations, convenience stores, RV parks and smoke shops. They sponsor and host many events which draw people to town. They are some of Butte County's biggest employers and some of PG&E's biggest accounts.

I was friends with the Tribal Chairman of the casino/hotel which the PG&E mistake was made on. Years ago we played golf and poker together and he was an occasional customer in my shop. When I heard the story about the two Small Claims Court victories, I visited him in his office. I was hoping he'd look into it, go for a refund and treat Lorraine and me to dinner at the Steak House for tipping him off.

He said he didn't even know about the mistake. He had me talk to the controller on his in-house phone. I asked him about PG&E's mistake and if there was a refund from the city. He said, "Oh yeah, I remember now that you mention it. We got a city check for $67,000 a while back, something about an overcharge." I thought I heard incorrectly. It seemed to me the $67,000 refund was probably enough for the whole ten years. I asked the Tribal Chairman, "How much you guys pay PG&E a month?" He said, sometimes it hits

$150,000. Those months the city would have mistakenly received $7,500 in illegal tax revenue from this single PG&E account. The Tribal Chairman thanked me and said he was going to look into it.

When I saw him a couple of months later I asked him if he was at liberty to say what happened. He said their attorney was researching it. He said the total amount for all the years which had not been refunded was $770,000. After several months went by, I saw him again. He said he didn't know why the attorney didn't want to go after it. I said, "Wow, I fought the city for a year for fifty bucks and you guys let three quarters of a million slip through the cracks." The free dinner I had in mind also slipped through the cracks. I've heard nothing else, not another word, for the past several years. He still stops by for a haircut once in a while. I decided it might be better to never mention it again.

One of my attorney customers had told me, at that time, Small Claims Court decisions do not set precedents for Superior Court cases.

Not being schooled in law, I imagined the Small Claim Court decisions would certainly deserve some consideration in a Superior Court hearing.

In my opinion, if the plaintiffs prevailed when challenging the very same defendant for the very same thing, and were awarded a small settlement, equal justice would only be served if the same conclusion was reached if the amount was large. What do I know? I've only been behind the iron chair for sixty years. I'm still trying to learn.

CHAPTER 10

Press Coverage, Incomplete or Biased?

If one attends city council meetings in person, many more details are observed when compared to watching them on video. Body language and facial expressions sometimes are more important than the verbiage. The problem is, ninety plus percent of the time you have to be able to withstand some boredom. You need patience. There have been times the newspaper only reports on one or two agenda items and doesn't even bother to write a single line on the others.

I don't like it when reporters focus on the fluff. In my opinion, way too often, they ignored the meat and potatoes, which should have been the lead story. Some actions which deserved the big bold headlines got no ink at all.

My letter to the editor which was printed 9/28/18, several weeks before the 2018 election pointed this out. Since it was the only letter I was allowed, due to the editor's one letter, per writer, limit, I wanted to throw an effective punch. Part of what I wrote… "I wish the marquee headline of the Oroville Mercury Register on February 21 had been Oroville City Council Violates Federal Law {followed by} *Last night Oroville City Council chose to violate federal law regarding cannabis by a vote of 5 to 2*. I wish the July 11, 2018, headline had been Oroville City Council Violates State Law (followed by) *Ignoring the advice of the city attorney, last night, Oroville City Council violated the Brown Act by voting to censure the mayor by a vote of 5-0. The same five councilors voted to violate federal law in February.* I believe those two actions deserved top billing, as they are the most defining decisions council has made this year."

I began writing this chapter the same day the local paper (5/26/20) had a story previewing some future fireworks coming to Oroville City Council Chambers. It made it sound like councilor Art Hatley is now on board with Linda Draper and Janet Goodson in bringing in outside law firms to assist if there is a grievance. A special council meeting was held the following day at 1:30. I watched it twice. Hatley denied contacting a legal firm. He claimed the first he heard about it was when the legal firm contacted him with some questions. Mayor Reynolds pointed out to Hatley, he should be enraged since his name appeared on the complaint in bold print. Hatley also made it clear if anyone from the council or staff asked him anything else, he would refuse to answer.

The meeting, along with the newspaper article of the following day sure confirmed the title of this chapter. I think the next day's paper left out the most important part of the story. Janet Goodson implied the four councilors, who are not among the MJ3, committed a crime. She seemed to believe the four conducted a closed door session when she, Draper, and Hatley were not present. That would have been a violation of the Brown Act. Goodson voiced another complaint. She said the other four serving on the council lacked transparency. Mayor Reynolds gave her the opportunity to use some transparency herself when he asked her who alerted her to the situation. She refused to answer, stating Journalism 101 teaches to not reveal sources. She's an elected representative, not a journalist. She vehemently complained about the lack of transparency in other councilors but must feel she, herself, is exempt from being transparent.

The reason there was a dispute and a special council meeting which led to the fireworks in the Council Chambers on 5/27/20 was because of the controversial California Voter Rights Act of 2001. There were differing opinions on whether or not the law was constitutional. The United States Supreme Court had this case coming up for consideration. The City of Oroville, along with some other California cities, had delivered written support for the challenging side of the argument. Goodson accused City Attorney Scott Huber of circumventing council approval. The City Attorney claimed legal protocol had been followed. Councilor Draper admitted she remembered some discussion of the matter at an earlier meeting. This acknowledgement was appreciated by Mayor Reynolds.

That same morning, before the council meeting even started, the United States Supreme Court denied to hear the case. Neither side in the Council Chambers pulled any punches just because the court battle was not to be. Serious verbal blows were still thrown.

Local political skirmishes pale in comparison to what we see in our federal legislative bodies on a daily basis. Capitol Hill has become a coliseum which hosts the team sport of Political Tug of War. If a great idea comes from the opposite side of the field, team members and fans hold their noses and point their thumbs down. Had the same exact idea been presented by their own side, there would be cheering, along with high praise and full support.

The national press coverage is much worse than we see locally. TV networks know their very survival depends on playing to their fans. Both biased reporting, and highlighting a very small portion of the entire picture, appeals to their loyal viewers. They leave out any part of the story which might shine a positive light for the other side. Sometimes only a single negative factor, out of ninety-nine other positive factors, receives any coverage. It doesn't matter. None of the good points ever get mentioned. I guess sometimes presenting fake news is necessary to keep a job. So be it. Some viewers can't even bring themselves to watch the networks which focus on the opposite side of their own viewpoints. Those people miss out on a lot. Sometimes they only get one percent of a story. I watch them all. That's how to get more of the picture.

It's been 52 years since we've had such shocking news stories. We're on track to surpass 1968. We opened 2020 with partisan politics rising to dizzying heights. We know of only one Senator who broke party ranks and voted for the other side after the impeachment trial. Some of his colleagues who hang the "R" behind their name's labeled him a traitor. Some of those with the "D" figured he is the only honest one in the entire other party. A bigger story was on the way.

Along came Covid 19. It took the spotlight. At least one of us had his longest break from working in 62 years. Government overstepped its boundaries for a country which touts freedom. Rather than make suggestions to a free society, federal, state and local restrictions were put in place. Career criminals were freed from jails. Their cells were soon to be occupied by defiant business people who broke the new law and opened up their businesses. Go figure.

The next story was even bigger yet. It had more impact. A policeman murdered a citizen. Even after murder charges were filed against the policeman, riots which included looting, arson, and assault spread throughout the nation. In 1965 I was treated to a tour of the Watts Riot, courtesy of California National Guard. Back then, we were assigned a duty. Stop the criminal anarchists. We did. Deadly force was authorized. Riots did not spread all over the country. The battle plan was to end it quickly. We did. It was not an election year. Unlike today, no political booty could be won by allowing looters to break, enter, and burn. I doubt I'll ever be able to understand how some politicians seem to have found reason to sympathize with protesters who commit serious crimes.

CHAPTER 11

Closing Potpourri

Back in the nineties, hair art made a little niche in barber history. Probably some creative barber and some willing young folks liked the idea of carving some close clipper lines into the sides of their haircuts. Soon came lightening bolts and later cartoon characters. An artistic minded teenager came in before flying to Disneyland. He'd drawn a picture of a haircut he wanted. It resembled a pronounced bowl cut. The big difference was this bowl cut had drooping V's. Imagine a sawtooth look, with giant saw-teeth. There is enough room on a head for seven sawtooth V's, two on each side and three on the back. This kid had light skin and dark hair, ideal for hair art.

When he got home from Disneyland he told me several people at the airport and on the plane asked if they could take his picture. He said at Disneyland, probably two hundred people didn't even ask. They just took his picture. I thought maybe a new trend had begun.

It never did catch on. Twenty some years later, in 2017, one of my friends pitched *Alaska Gold Rush* TV producers to do a *California Gold Rush* episode. His family had a placer gold mine for most of his life. He was willing to meet the requirements to do a show.

I tried to persuade him to let me put a *sawtooth bowl cut* on him for the TV show. He declined. Being of middle age and already having senior citizen hair color didn't really matter. He was one who darkened his hair with dye. The sawtooth look would show up just fine. I joked with him, the haircut would enhance his natural goofy looks and he could wind up just as famous as *The Three Stooges*.

The same series of wet storms which took out the Oroville Dam Spillway in 2017 caused land slides which had to be dealt with before mining could begin. Three years got by. I talked to him in April of 2020. A couple of weeks earlier, the Gold Rush crew spent some time at his mine filming. *California Gold Rush*, featuring my friend, at least has some chance of making the show. If he had the sawtooth haircut, it would have been a sure thing.

Back in the nineties, a teenager came in with a magazine which had a picture of a logo of some youth group. I didn't care about the meaning of the logo, I just needed to see if I could figure out how to carve it in the back of his head. It took a long time, but it came out really good. He was beaming when he saw it in the mirror. When Mom came back to pick him up, he proudly showed her the carving and asked her if she knew the meaning of the logo. I loved her one word response. With shoulders shrugged, she asked, "Ignorance?"

Another good hair art story was about a high school senior with a job, a car and a lot of freedom. For some reason, unknown to me, he wanted me to write, 'NOW RENTING' around his head.

This is about all the letters you have room for. His black hair made it easy to read. The same night the police found reason to take him and one of his friends in for questioning. They were very inquisitive about the meaning of the writing on his head. He told me, one cop said it was sure easy to tell there was a vacancy.

One of my schoolteacher customers had gone a little too long between haircuts. When he finally made it in, it was right in the middle of a school day. This might have been back in the eighties. He liked the standard gentlemanly hair cut with a nice blended taper up the back.

I left him an inch wide tail which really stood out in the middle of a short taper. I didn't offer him a look in the mirror. Back on the job, when he turned towards the blackboard during the next class, all the kids started snickering. He turned back around and felt his back-seam thinking there could be a rip. He and I both have expanded senses of humor. When he came back after school to get the haircut finished we both had a good laugh.

A few years later he brought his little girl in with him. She liked a little boy at school who had a flat-top with lightening bolts carved in the sides. She wanted a haircut like that too. Without his wife's knowledge, he let her get one. After I was finished, the little girl was looking in the mirror grinning. I wouldn't have wanted to be him when he got home and the Mom saw. He squeaked out of it. He blamed it on me. She probably believed him, remembering the haircut with a tail.

There's a lot more to barbering than putting out quality hair-cuts. It is good to be able to do this when the need arises. Remembering from 1960, the first thing they teach you in Barber College is to never say *whoops*. They grade haircuts on balance and even-ness. But, the only person who gets to decide if the haircut is good or bad is your customer. Sometimes when the Mom over-rules the customer, teardrops fall to the floor along with the locks of hair. It's not much fun when this happens.

With a new customer, it's very important to communicate before starting in order to try to figure out how to proceed. Some of us feel understanding exactly what the customer wants should be crystal clear before starting. Sometimes you have to change the communication channel several times before you're able to get on the same page. Sometimes confusion builds with everything they say. You never really get there. Everyone communicates in a differ-ent manner. The sixty year education in human nature has some advantages. You come to realize we are all different. What some see as logical, others see as ridiculous.

I've probably seen hundreds of haircuts leave my shop hoping no potential customers are watching. If they see something which looks bad, they avoid ever giving you a shot. If you see people running out of a restaurant vomiting, you never go in.

When we, the four oldest barbers in town were all past seventy, most of our clients were also senior citizens. Many seniors don't put a quality haircut at the top of the list when choosing a barber. They have a preference for the flavor of B.S. (not Barber Shop) which is usually bandied around in each different shop. Some guys would stop in to visit when they didn't need a haircut. They just wanted a serving of '*poop du jour*.' One of the four old barbers did hunting and fishing, one had an impressive car collection, I featured local politics, and the fourth had a potty mouth. Some old guys would request "Haircut only please, no B.S." This kind, usually just stopped in at a shop which had no line-up.

In *Headscratchers & Boondoggles, 1) First ... the Worst*, I mentioned a friend phoned and alerted me, my name was mentioned at a council meeting. Many of our customers become close friends, like family. Several have been customers and friends for over 50 years. The one who called me that day is one of those.

Back in '66, as a 23 year old newlywed, I was lucky enough to become a self employed barber. I was invited to buy a piece of the King's Men Barber Shop, which had replaced Fischer's as the biggest, busiest shop in town. Sam Pattison, the friend who had called me was a little kid at the time. His family lived in the residential area close to our shop. Sam, his brother and Dad usually all got haircuts at the same time. It was a family affair. Mom and sister would usually be there too. The whole neighborhood was happy when his sister, Patty, was named *Little Miss Oroville*. Back then, almost all of our customers seemed to respect the presence of polite company and refrained from the usual colorful language.

King's Men specialized in jokes and pranks. Every week or two a customer would ask "Who was that fellow that just left?" We were ready. The answer was loud enough so everyone in the shop could hear, "I don't know, but he left behind this silver bullet." The barbers would all start humming William Tell's Overture (Lone Ranger's theme song). Then one of us would yell, *"Where does the Lone Ranger take his garbage? Toooo da dump, to da dump, to da dump... to da dump, dump, dump"* we'd all sing. Occasionally, this kind of humor would cost us a customer.

When Sam and his friends became old enough to be running around, they'd stop in just to visit and see what kind of funny stuff was going on. When the whole family was there, Sam never took a peek at one of the *Playboy* magazines which were in the racks of most barber shops. I don't think he was that careful when he was there, just with his buddies.

FINAL COMMENTS

I am thankful and blessed because of my life's experiences. Sixty years of standing behind a barber chair and learning things from all segments of society gives one a very special education. One day you get to hear a Hatfield complain about the McCoys, and the next day you get to hear a McCoy complain about the Hatfields. Everyday you get to hear the **"D's"** blame the evil **"R's"** for everything wrong with the country and the **"R's"** blame the evil **"D's"** for the same thing.

All levels of government have a segment of elected representatives which put their own philosophy and agenda at the top of the priority list. If legal restrictions are in the way, some devise clever ways to circumvent them and actually succeed in getting through undetected. Some of these seem to think they are entitled to turn around and point to the twig of mistletoe pinned on their shirt-tails, when questioned by citizens. Others, lacking in cleverness, seem to obliviously stumble along, causing many constituents to wonder whether or not they know what they're doing, and seriously doubt they should even be serving. Luckily, a third segment of the elected actually are honorable people. This mixture leads to friction. Both the "R's" and "D's" have some of each. As long as the honorable are in the majority, it does not matter. It seems to me, way too often, the honorable are in the minority.

My opinions are based on my observations and my unique life's experiences. This is one thing we all have in common. Our convictions are formed as we journey through life on our own, totally diverse, individual paths.

In some countries people can be incarcerated and even executed for criticizing their government. We are lucky to live in America. We have the right to call them out. That is freedom. *America is great.*

Any resemblance To Any Other Works Is Unintentional